HOT TOPICS

IN THE

LEGAL

PROFESSION

~

2010

Benefit Tulane PILF Series

Quid Pro Law Books
New Orleans, Louisiana

Hot Topics in the Legal Profession ~ 2010

The *Benefit Tulane PILF Series* of law books helps to fund the school's public interest organization and the placements it sponsors for the representation of indigent clients and public causes. More information is found in the Foreword.

Compilation and Foreword copyright © 2010 by Steven Alan Childress. All rights reserved. No copyright is claimed as to statutory materials, judicial decisions or ethics rules quoted herein. Copyright to the individual chapters is owned by their respective authors and Quid Pro, LLC, and published here with their permission. No material in this book may be reproduced, copied or retransmitted in any manner without the written consent of the publisher.

Published in 2010 by Quid Pro Law Book. Printed in the United States of America.

ISBN-10: 1610279905
ISBN-13: 9781610279901

Quid Pro, LLC
5860 Citrus Blvd., Suite D-101
New Orleans, Louisiana 70123
www.quidprolaw.com

qp

Publisher's Cataloging-in-Publication

Childress, Steven Alan (ed.).

    Hot Topics in the Legal Profession 2010 / by Steven Alan Childress (ed.).

    p. cm.

ISBN-13: 9781610279901 (paperback edition)
ISBN-13: 9780982750452 (digital ebook edition)
ISBN-13: 9781452356204 (digital multiformat and ePub edition)

"A timely collection of student studies on current events in legal ethics and the U.S. legal profession, discussing issues both important and changing during 2009-2010."

1. Law—United States. 2. Attorney and client—United States. 3. The legal profession. 4. Legal ethics. I. Title.

HOT TOPICS IN THE LEGAL PROFESSION

~

2010

---

edited by Steven Alan Childress

Quid Pro Law Books
www.quidprolaw.com

Table of Contents

FOREWORD: ON ETHICS AND THE PROFESSION IN A TIME OF CHALLENGE AND CHANGE i

ABOUT THE EDITOR AND AUTHORS vii

Hot Topics in the Legal Profession ~ 2010 1

    Chapter 1: Intersecting the First Amendment, Ethics, and the Internet: Memo to Other States from the Louisiana Experience 1

    Chapter 2: "Friends," Episode 1: The Ethical Pitfalls of Lawyers Getting "Friendly" Online 17

    Chapter 3: "Friends," Episode 2: The Wisdom of Discretionary Recusal and the Judge as Actual Friend 31

    Chapter 4: "Friends," Episode 3: Appearance of Impropriety, Judges on Facebook, and the Modern Day Contact Rolodex 43

    Chapter 5: The Problem of Circumventing the Labor Management Reporting and Disclosure Act by Using the Ancillary Business Model 55

    Chapter 6: Canary in a Coal Mine: How *Caperton v. A.T. Massey Coal Co.* Demonstrates the Need for Oxygen and Reform in State Supreme Courts 67

    Chapter 7: Negotiation Ethics: Balancing Ethically Permissible Conduct with Integrity and Professionalism in Settlement Talks 83

ABOUT THIS BOOK 92

To the members of Tulane Public Interest Law Foundation

and the public-minded students it sponsors

FOREWORD

ON ETHICS AND THE PROFESSION IN A TIME OF CHALLENGE AND CHANGE

Although dilemmas of ethics and philosophy have been around since ancient Greece, many issues of modern legal ethics move at lightning speed. Legal ethics and professional responsibility are not static mandates but rather use evolving concepts and rules. The year 2009, and carrying into the first half of 2010, confirmed this reality yet again. For instance, the American Bar Association hotly debated and eventually passed some significant amendments to its Model Rules of Professional Conduct, notably in the areas of conflicts of interest — particularly permitting Rule 1.10 "screening" of an attorney who changes jobs from preventing her own disqualification to impute to the entire firm or office she joined. These and other rules changes and tweaks are starting to take hold in the many state bar organizations which actually put the ABA recommendations into effect, all while many more states are implementing the last round of wholesale revision to the Model Rules which the ABA finalized in 2002 as part of its "Ethics 2000" project. (For example, New York, on April 1, 2009 (?!), finally became a "rules" state, more or less, and California took steps toward abandoning its traditional use of the ABA's earlier Model Code of Professional Responsibility.)

More change is on the way from the ABA and state bar rules' committees, some of it eventually to come from the new Commission on Ethics 20/20, formed in 2009. That committee of leading lawyers, judges, and academics likely will offer some profound rule changes long before the decade closes, perhaps defying a corollary I would add to Parkinson's Law: work, and deadlines, expand to match the name of the project if you stick what looks like a date on it. And, anyway, all of this is just about that slice of legal ethics involving the ABA's proposed amendments and the various states' ultimate acceptance or rejection of the model.

Real change came in that slice, in 2009, but it is only part of the story of legal ethics in 2009-2010. This is because ethical guidelines, as important as they are especially when implemented by state bars and courts, would mean little if not enforced. It is in the bar discipline structures and state courts on review (and less directly by state and federal courts themselves in disciplining or sanctioning attorneys before them, by citing the ethics rules as grounds) that much of the action takes place. To know the law of lawyering, one must look past the promulgated rules, even the state-specific versions, and survey the bar decisions and the discipline actually imposed, to see ethics standards have bite and even evolve. Court review of judicial decisions is also instructive, both in setting forth what the rules mean in that jurisdiction and in getting a feel for the kind of punishment typically imposed for certain misconduct. This is also true for judicial ethics: the latest versions of the ABA's Judicial Code tells part of the story, but its implementation in state organizations and courts tells the all-important ending. All of these areas saw some interesting developments over the past year.

Beyond rules of conduct and their enforcement by bar organizations and judges, there is a whole world of law governing lawyers that is simply not about bar discipline or sanctions. This includes legislative enactments that affect lawyers and their conduct (either exclusively, as with state law changes to accepted contingency fee caps, or in a wide net of other professionals and legal actors, such as financial disclosure laws). These sometimes contravene an ethics rule. This world also includes judicial decisions and other law affecting professional liability, especially legal malpractice for professional failure, redressed in private civil lawsuits by clients and in similar actions for breach of fiduciary duties. As case law decides the rules of malpractice and enforces them through sometimes-expensive decisions, so the world of the law about lawyers evolves some more, here in the common law way. The relevant period is known for some famous malpractice actions, notably including a $72 million jury verdict in May 2009 against Akin Gump in a patent matter.

Moreover, that is just the changing world of professional regulation, governance, and liability in the United States. The matter gets much bigger, and the changes even more pronounced, once one considers the legal profession in all its structural, economic and social upheaval during this time: law firm layoffs and deferments, major partner moves, the effect on legal education of reform ideas and recession reality (combined with mounting student debt), the shrinking of traditional law work and moving it in-house or abroad, and of course lawyer happiness, satisfaction and—in many situations—desperation. Also, the lawyer picture, and the changes in 2009-2010, grow further when one ventures outside the U.S. and looks at changes the world over, in a time of recession, outsourcing, and corporatizing of law firms. These stories and more dominated the headlines of the law media over the past two years, and they promise to continue to highlight massive adaptation to come.

All of this is to say that there is a lot of "law of lawyering" out there, and even more economic and social issues in the legal profession beyond law as such. For each specific example, one could write a book. I have not done so. But I have collected some excellent essays from Tulane law students written in 2010 about legal and judicial ethics, and have bundled them into this book on current events. I offer it not as a survey of the entirety of the field of ethics and the profession, but as a "selected topics" book, admittedly of some of the most pressing and fascinating topics this year. The students chose the topics, either as an independent study they devised and wrote, or as part of the writing requirements for an advanced seminar in legal ethics. Yet by and large, I think that they chose . . . wisely, to allude to the third Indiana Jones film. These are some great topics, with current application and meaning, and I hope that lawyers, judges, and academics — as well as the general public interested in lawyers' roles and rules — find them to be useful, as I did. Not every profound event in the profession is purported to be represented here, as it might in a blog over time or in a comprehensive survey, but the topics explored here matter, and the students' research and views will be useful to note.

Anyone trying to keep up lately with the state of flux in legal ethics, and the profession writ large, will find some helpful tools in digital form, among them updated law blogs. In particular, the best sources for really current events are *The Legal Profession Blog* and *Legal Ethics Forum*. Both blogs have been named to the *ABA*

Journal's "Top 100 Law Blogs" for all three years it has picked. And about these two blogs, *Capital Defense Weekly* once wrote, "as someone who is petrified of effing up and losing the bar card, these sites are tops of my RSS feeds." Not to slight the other editors of these blogs (including me, writing for LPB), but as to hot topics, I would say that the standout and prolific work of Michael Frisch (LPB) and John Steele (LEF), in particular, will keep any lawyer or bar observer current as to the state of the profession, rules changes, and discipline reports. John tallies up the "top ten legal ethics stories" of the year each December, in an awesome list on LEF, in addition to his regular insightful contributions and observations. And Mike at LPB publishes summaries and comments on bar reports, often three or four times *every day*, bringing to bear his previous experience as a bar prosecutor and his prodigious research into all the state bars and courts. Between them, and their stories, reports, and opinions on the subject, you are covered for late-breaking news in the area of legal ethics and professional liability. On the other hand, it was LPB blogger Nancy Rapoport who uncovered this jaw-dropping gem in April 2010, as the Pennsylvania state bar's e-newsletter reported:

> Also, 12 attorneys paid their annual fees with checks marked as drawn on a trust or escrow account, prompting an immediate inquiry from Disciplinary Counsel.[2] Eighty-seven paid with checks drawn on insufficient funds; four of which were still outstanding at press time. Not smart.

And, Nancy added, "footnote 2 itself is classic: '2. The ethical equivalent of a "Please kick me" sign.'"

There are other sources out there that help keep readers updated too: for example, general purpose law blogs featuring occasional reports on ethics, the *ABA Journal*'s own blog, and the quarterly newsletters of the AALS Section on Professional Responsibility (which they allow me to post to LPB, so it is easily found by a site search). Writers and practitioners in the field are lucky to have these resources.

In looking back at both blogs over the past six months, I note that some of the chapters in this book were nicely foreshadowed. John's year-end roundup on legal ethics mentioned some topics covered here (e.g., judicial ethics and campaign contributions, social websites), as well as big stories not covered here (revising Rule 1.10 imputation, the economy and layoffs, criminal prosecution of defense attorneys). Similarly, among other interesting or surprising bar stories he covered, Mike was first to break nationally with the issue of whether judges can make Facebook "friends," a social networking dilemma given disparate treatment, he noted, in South Carolina and Florida. You can count on it being an issue that must be resolved in 48 other states, because social networking is not going away and yet the "appearance of impropriety" is suggested by some forms of virtual social contact.

Those interested in that dilemma, and the initial reaction in those two states, should read Chapter 4 by Renee Goudeau, discussing the appearance of impropriety rule and its application to judicial networking. Chapter 3 by Daniel Meyer fits nicely with that, exploring the more general ethical dilemma of judges having lawyer friends. Not Facebook friends — real ones. Again the reach of impropriety's appearance, versus the reality of everyday social situations, makes for an issue worth exploring. More generally, in chapter 2, Lara Richards studies the *lawyer* ethics issues of social networking and internet interaction — as well as deception in using Facebook to find smoking guns on adverse parties — and she details very recent opinions and decisions on these subjects. The direction from the ABA and state bars is as yet unclear, she notes. To me, the unhelpful and sometimes outmoded advice that lawyers are now given by their regulators is the bar equivalent of one Facebook category of marital status: "It's complicated."

Related, in that new technology brings new ethics challenges, is our Chapter 1 by Brittany Buckley, as she discusses the use of the internet to market and advertise. She details the very recent judicial histories of efforts in Louisiana and Florida to restrict internet advertising, and more broadly to control many other forms of new media, television, and radio advertising. One court has sustained some parts and nixed others, so this issue too is not going away soon — in fact, her paper details ways in which the same issue can arise right now in some 23 other states. One can anticipate that many state bars will follow suit, while other lawsuits will lead to judicial review of measures already in place, very much like the decision she explores here.

Another area in which the clarity and helpfulness of the Model Rules falls short in actual practice is in the dilemma of truthfulness and deception in negotiations. In Chapter 7, Camalla Kimbrough analyzes the topic under the general rules on truth and advocacy, and in the process highlights some competing scholarly and judicial views on the subject, including some who try to incorporate personal integrity and professionalism into the settlement process.

One ethical dilemma that is about to expand in importance is the role of lawyers and their ancillary nonlawyer consulting businesses under recent changes to the Labor-Management Reporting and Disclosure Act. In Chapter 5, Ryan Lopatka notes the new direction of the LMRDA under the Obama administration and anticipates that it will foment such ancillary entities, to avoid the act's disclosure requirements under a special exemption. This will in turn raise troubling issues about the ethical obligations of the lawyers involved, all ultimately returning to the question of whether or not the ancillary wing falls under lawyer rules (for example, in terms of advertising and Rule 1.8(a) client waiver). The law in other similar situations is mixed, he notes, and Ryan offers his view of how these questions might be resolved specifically for the newer LMRDA. Even those not concerned about labor law and campaign disclosures will find his analysis useful for any effort to form an ancillary business under a law firm umbrella.

Perhaps the biggest ethics story of 2009 was the Supreme Court's decision in *Caperton v. A.T. Massey Coal Co.*, dealing with campaign finance of judges, judicial recusal, and due process concerns (John in fact ranked it story #1). Chapter 6 by Elizabeth Adams analyzes the decision and discusses the questions it raises more generally about judicial selection and recusal, including policy proposals which undoubtedly should be addressed by legislatures over the next few years. Massey ultimately won the case in West Virginia anyway: Elizabeth tells, as Paul Harvey would say, "the *rest* of the story," something interesting even for those who have read the case or some previous articles written about it. Regardless, the whole process should be a wake-up call for judicial elections, retention, and accountability. The even more current tie-in to the story? It was a Massey mine that just two months ago blew up and killed several mine workers.

These are the topics explored in this volume. Each contribution was solicited from student work observed during the spring 2010 semester at Tulane Law School, from two sources: (1) a seminar on Civil Litigation Ethics, offered by Larry Feldman, Jr., a partner at McGlinchey Stafford on our adjunct faculty, and (2) my supervision of independent studies researched and written by students interested in the subject. Because I decided to compile them into this collection after my students turned in papers (in part as a positive reaction), keep in mind that they wrote them for that academic purpose. I know that they succeeded with their target audience, yet I believe that they will be interesting and useful to a broader audience too. But to be fair to these students, please note that I never talked to them about that larger use until after the fact (or about, for that matter, the Bluebook or typical law review formatting and style). This is not to suggest that they do not succeed on those measures too; I could not possibly know, as the last time I saw a Bluebook, Al Gore had not yet invented the internet any more than *Harvard Law Review* editors like Barack Obama and Elena Kagan had ciphered a way to cite it. I still have not talked to them about the Bluebook and do not intend to (more important to me was adapting their notes to the digital format, with its own universe of rules, and errors in that are mine, not the students'). Traditional perfection was not the purpose of their work but my reaction to these brief papers was simply that, both in substance and in format, they ought to be read by more than just me.

I suspect the same is true of those contributions from Larry's seminar: they had a target and goal in mind, not this book, yet the result was a product that Larry and I agreed would be useful in practice, courts, and schools. In reviewing them, I appreciated the level of execution too. (I do recall mentioning the idea of a student book to a professor elsewhere and caught his look of horror. All while I am thinking, hmm, for decades students have decided which professors get tenure by selecting articles to publish; this ebook idea seemed less perverse to me.) I know that Larry asked them to interject personal opinion and reflection into their topics — how would they react if *they* were in that situation? — and his students did so; I liked that, and left it in for the reader to consider, again without *my* considering whether a law review editor would countenance such a question. I very much appreciate that Larry shared his views of the potential contributions, and that the students so selected generously shared their papers for this project. For more on all the students (many of them now *graduates*), see *About the Authors*, following this Foreword.

There was another purpose as well. That is, this volume is the initial work in the *Benefit Tulane PILF Series* — the first I hope of many — and its net proceeds benefit our school's organization, the Public Interest Law Foundation (which is not, I must add, responsible for any content or errors). Tulane PILF is a non-profit whose student members work tirelessly to promote legal representation of indigent clients and public interest causes, throughout the United States, by funding internships of students in law jobs for that purpose. PILF members sell coffee and treats each morning (Diet Dr. Pepper for me, they already know); they run a fantastic and entertaining auction each spring; and they perform many other labor-intensive services throughout the year. All just to help their classmates have great public interest work experiences, and to help clients who need representation by the brilliant and eager young minds we can offer them.

Those needs—clients needing legal help, public-minded students needing support for work—are more acute than ever. Yet PILF can only sell so much coffee and the loathsome Skittles (so looking like an M&M but so not). This book series, and the *extra donations* that may come from readers of PILF's web page, is offered in part to fund that need and remind people of the sacrifice and excitement for this cause that so many students at Tulane bring to bear when they volunteer for PILF. Whether the book succeeds on that level is entirely up to you.

Look for more book collections to come in the *Benefit Tulane PILF Series*, in other fields of law, and again on legal ethics in 2011. Find new ones to download and read (even on PC, Mac, BlackBerry, Androids, iPhone, and iPad apps) by searching "Tulane PILF" in Amazon's Kindle store (or qpbooks.com). And please propose your own collection of student, lawyer, or professor works for the Series, for instance if you are a scholar who would like to publish digitally the proceedings of a themed panel that you organized for a conference (the papers themselves may become published elsewhere as articles, of course, or posted to SSRN, while the edited collection as a whole, with the organizer's Foreword about the panel's subject and purpose, would be published digitally in the Series). Sponsoring Tulane PILF may be the best way to get such interconnected, cutting-edge academic studies *out there* fast, or to make sure that quality student work becomes useful to a broader audience — as we have tried to do in this book.

In addition to acknowledging Larry Feldman, Jr. and the current president of PILF, Vivie Satorsky (along with her board, who brainstormed quickly on this notion while they should have been studying for finals), I wish to thank colleagues at Tulane who offered ideas for the project, including Vice Dean Jancy Hoeffel and our other two ethics professors, Pamela Metzger and Robert Westley.

—Steven Alan Childress

New Orleans, Louisiana
May 2010

ABOUT THE EDITOR AND AUTHORS

Steven Alan Childress is the Conrad Meyer III Professor of Law at Tulane, where he teaches legal ethics, torts, and evidence. He earned his law degree from Harvard and a Ph.D. in Jurisprudence & Social Policy from Berkeley. He is an editor of The Legal Profession Blog and a member of the California and D.C. bars. Alan coauthored Federal Standards of Review (LexisNexis, 2010).

Elizabeth A. Adams is a member of the Tulane Class of 2011. After graduating cum laude from Rice, she moved to France where she worked as a paralegal with Baker & McKenzie before starting law school. At Tulane, Elizabeth is Senior Articles Editor for the Tulane Journal of International and Comparative Law, and during her third year she will extern with the United States Attorney's Office for the Eastern District of Louisiana.

Brittany L. Buckley graduated in May 2010 from Tulane Law School and is preparing to practice in Louisiana, as she is currently studying for the Louisiana bar. She is a 2007 graduate of Virginia Tech, in Political Science and Spanish.

Renee Goudeau graduated cum laude from Tulane Law School in May 2010 with the Civil Law Certificate, and previously earned her B.A. degree in Communications from LSU. While in law school, she was a member of Civil Law Commentaries. Renee has interned for two federal judges and clerked for a law firm in her home town of Shreveport, Louisiana.

Camalla Kimbrough graduated from Duke in 2008 with a B.A. in Psychology. She is in Tulane Law's Class of 2011. Camalla has published Note, "Launch Away: Second Circuit Rules that Degree of User Influence Determines Whether a Webcasting Service Must Obtain Individual Licenses for Performing Sound Recordings," 12 Tul. J. Tech. & Intell. Prop. 293 (2009), and has a Comment in that journal on the NFL forthcoming in 2011.

J. Ryan Lopatka earned his J.D. in May 2010 from Tulane, and is presently living in his home town of Chicago. He holds a B.A. in History from Loyola, N.O. In law school, Ryan has specialized in international trade and securities law. He participated in Tulane's summer schools in London and Cambridge, and interned with UBS in London.

Daniel Meyer is a May 2010 law graduate of Tulane. He is currently interning in Orleans Parish Criminal Court while studying for the bar. A native of Atlanta, he attended the University of Georgia (B.A. 2007), and has clerked for law firms and the SEC. During law school, Daniel worked in the Civil Litigation Clinic, won an Intraschool Moot Court competition, chaired Tulane's Invitational Moot Court tournament, and studied admiralty law in Greece.

Lara K. Richards is a member of the Class of 2011 at Tulane and a managing editor of the Tulane Law Review. Before law school, she graduated from Notre Dame in 1997 and was a journalist with a Texas newspaper. Thus summer she is clerking for firms in New York and New Orleans. In her third year, Lara will be externing for the U.S. Attorney's Office in New Orleans.

Chapter 1

Intersecting the First Amendment, Ethics, and the Internet: Memo to Other States from the Louisiana Experience

Brittany L. Buckley

After nearly four years of drafting, public hearings, and litigation, the Louisiana Supreme Court finally implemented amended rules of professional conduct which heavily regulate lawyer advertising in Louisiana. Effective October 1, 2009, the seventeen pages of new Louisiana lawyer advertising rules[1] generated conflict and confusion among members of the bar before the rules were ever implemented. In its zealous yet well-intentioned effort to strictly regulate lawyer advertising, in whatever form, Louisiana prompted the *Public Citizen, Inc. v. Louisiana Attorney Disciplinary Board*[2] lawsuit ("*Public Citizen*"). In this lawsuit, several Louisiana lawyers successfully challenged the Louisiana's complicated, expensive, and bureaucratic filing system for monitoring lawyer advertising on the Internet.

The *Public Citizen* case, while protracted and undoubtedly expensive for Louisiana to defend, raises important issues about the intersection of the internet, legal ethics rules, and the First Amendment. At a minimum, the Louisiana experience contributes to the ongoing conversation about the First Amendment's relationship to all kinds of speech on the internet. More importantly, *Public Citizen* challenges an assumption underlying the codes of professional conduct enforced in many states—the assumption that the internet is sufficiently analogous to television or print media such that applying the same rules designed for television or print media to the internet complies with the First Amendment. These questions raised in *Public Citizen*, and the mixed result in court and the aftermath of the litigation, should prompt other states both to carefully review their existing internet advertising restrictions and to methodically and narrowly craft such regulations in the future.

I. Background

    A. Why Reform in Louisiana?

Prior to the push for reform, Louisiana already prohibited any false, misleading, or deceptive advertisements.[3] Louisiana also specifically prohibited some specific advertising practices such as comparing the lawyer's services with the services of another lawyer or law firm, and implying the ability to unlawfully influence any tribunal.[4] Still, some members of the bar vocally denounced certain permissible

---

[1] *See* Louisiana State Bar Association, "New Lawyer Advertising Rules, effective 10-01-2009," *available at* http://www.lsba.org/2007MemberServices/Advert0609/LA%20Rule%207-1%20through%207-10%20(2008%20eff%2010-01-2009%20amended%202006-30-2009%20-%20noting%2009-22-09%20Order)%20(2).pdf.
[2] 642 F. Supp. 2d 539 (E.D. La. 2009).
[3] *See* Louisiana Rule of Prof'l Conduct Rule 7.1(a) (2006).
[4] *See* Louisiana Rule of Prof'l Conduct Rule 7.1(a)(iii), (iv) (2006).

practices and the negative impact they perceived these practices to have on the view of the profession and the quality of legal services available to Louisianans.[5]

Responding to these concerns, the Louisiana State Bar Association had considered updating Louisiana lawyer advertising rules prior to Hurricane Katrina.[6] Yet the bar association's fear that the Louisiana legislature might usurp the bar's own control over the regulation of lawyer advertising served as the ultimate catalyst for the recent changes.[7] During the Louisiana legislature's 2006 session, Senator Maroinneaux sponsored Senate Bill 617, in which he attempted to create a Senate Standing Committee on Attorney Advertising and implement a screening process for all lawyer advertisements broadcast in Louisiana.[8] Bill 617, if enacted, would have essentially implemented the then-existing Florida lawyer advertising rules.[9] The bill, dubbed by one Louisiana lawyer as "legislation which [Senator Marionneaux] expressed . . . that he knew to be unconstitutional" and introduced only as at attempt at "personal retribution by Senator Marionneaux against my firm,"[10] was ultimately referred to Senate Judiciary Committee A.[11]

Perhaps recognizing complaints that Senator Marrionneax's proposal was a "heavy-handed attack by the legislature on an area that the Supreme Court clearly has jurisdiction over,"[12] the House rejected the bill. Ultimately, the Louisiana legislature adopted a concurrent resolution which recognized that "the manner in which some

---

[5] *See, e.g.,* Transcript of *Louisiana State Bar Association Public Hearing in re: Re-Evaluating Louisiana's Lawyer Advertising Rules*, November 16, 2006 (Shreveport) (hereinafter "Transcript of Shreveport Hearing"), at 23:7-41:2 (comments of Jack Bailey).

[6] Transcript of *Louisiana State Bar Association Public Hearing in re: Re-Evaluating Louisiana's Lawyer Advertising Rules*, November 9, 2006 (New Orleans) (hereinafter "Transcript of New Orleans Hearing"), at 3:12-3:17 (comments of Richard Stanley, Chair of Louisiana State Bar Professional Conduct Committee).

[7] Transcript of New Orleans Hearing, at 113:5-114:13 (statement of Richard Stanley) (noting that the impetus for reform was coming from the legislature and that the bar's failure to satisfactorily reform the advertising rules may cause the bar to lose its opportunity to have any input in the process); Transcript of *Louisiana State Bar Association Public Hearing in re: Re-Evaluating Louisiana's Lawyer Advertising Rules*, November 2, 2006 (Baton Rouge) (hereinafter "Transcript of Baton Rouge Hearing"), 7:23-11:18 (statement of Richard Lemmler, Ethics Counsel for Louisiana State Bar Association) (noting that the catalyst for the new lawyer advertising rules was a March, 2006 bill in the Louisiana State Senate).

[8] *See* Sen. Bill 617, 360th Leg., Reg. Sess. (La. 2006).

[9] Transcript of New Orleans Hearing at 113:12-15 (statement of Richard Stanley).

[10] Transcript of New Orleans Hearing at 114:15-24 (statement of Eric Guirard). It is worth noting that the Louisiana Supreme Court permanently disbarred Mr. Guirard in 2009 for permitting non-lawyers to handle his personal injury cases and violating the client solicitation rules, among other things. *See In re* E. Eric Guirard & Thomas P. Pittenger, 04-DB-005, Recommendation to the Louisiana Supreme Court, *available at* http://www.ladb.org/NXT/gateway.dll/DB/2008-11-06_04-DB-005.pdf?f=templates$fn=default.htm$vid=ladb:ladbview. *See also* Jim Shannon, "E. Eric Guirard 'E Guarantee' disbarred," May 5, 2009, *available at* http://www.wafb.com/Global/story.asp?S=10308078.

[11] *See* La. Sen. 2006 Reg. Session Instrument Information, SB 617- Regular Sessions 2006, *available at* http://www.legis.state.la.us/billdata/History.asp?sessionid=06RS&billid=SB617.

[12] Transcript of New Orleans Hearing at 115:2-4 (statement of Eric Guirard); *see also* Transcript of Shreveport Hearing at 3:5-10.

members of the Louisiana State Bar Association are advertising their services in this state has become undignified"[13] and asked the Louisiana Supreme Court to form a committee to review the lawyer advertising rules.[14]

B. The Revision Process

The Supreme Court formed the Committee to Study Attorney Advertising ("Supreme Court Committee").[15] The Supreme Court Committee, in turn, delegated much of this task to the to the already-existing Louisiana State Bar Association (LSBA) Rules of Professional Conduct Committee ("LSBA Committee").[16] The LSBA Committee would ultimately provide the vast majority of the manpower and other resources necessary to draft the new rules.[17] The LSBA Committee met four times between September 21, 2006 and October 6, 2006, and designed numerous proposed amendments to Part 7 of the Louisiana Rules of Professional conduct (which governs lawyer advertising). From the LSBA's point of view, the push to overhaul the advertising rules was, in large part, motivated by the concern to restrict certain advertisement practices on television.[18]

When it began the revision process in September of 2006, The LSBA Committee opted against starting from scratch.[19] Instead, the LSBA Committee began by carefully reviewing Rules of Professional Conduct already in place elsewhere.[20] In drafting the amendments to the Louisiana rules, the LSBA Committee decided to model the new Louisiana rules after the Florida rules on lawyer advertising.[21] By this time, scholars and even the United States Supreme Court had recognized Florida's "special distrust for electronic media advertising by lawyers"[22] and propensity to "push the First Amendment envelope."[23]

---

[13] *See* Transcript of Shreveport Hearing at 3:5-14.
[14] *Id.* at 3:12-19 (comments of Larry Shea, member of Louisiana State Bar Association Advertising Committee). *See also* Transcript of New Orleans Hearing at 113:15-21 (statement of Richard Stanley).
[15] *Id.* at 3:12-19 (comments of Larry Shea and Richard Lemmler).
[16] *See id.* at 3:30-4:5 (comments of Larry Shea).
[17] *See id.* at 3:1-11:21 (comments of Larry Shea).
[18] *Cf.* Transcript of Shreveport hearing at 23:7-41:2 (comments of Jack Bailey).
[19] Transcript of *Louisiana State Bar Association Public Hearing in re: Re-Evaluating Louisiana's Lawyer Advertising Rules*, November 8, 2006 (Lafayette) (hereinafter "Transcript of Lafayette Hearing"), at 10:21-23.
[20] *See* Transcript of Baton Rouge Hearing at 10:11-15 (statement of Richard Lemmler).
[21] Transcript of *Louisiana State Bar Association Public Hearing in re: Re-Evaluating Louisiana's Lawyer Advertising Rules*, November 2, 2006 (Baton Rouge) (hereinafter "Baton Rouge Public Hearing"), 7:23-11:18 (statement of Richard Lemmler, Ethics Counsel for Louisiana State Bar Association) (noting that the catalyst for the new lawyer advertising rules was a March, 2006 bill in the Louisiana State Senate, in which the Legislature focused on Florida's lawyer advertising rules and that "the subcommittee for the Rules of Professional Conduct Committee . . . decided that it would focus on Florida's Rules").
[22] Rodney A. Smolla, 1 Law of Lawyer Advertising § 7.21 (2009).
[23] Lyrissa Barnett Lidsky & Tera Jckowski Peterson, *Medium-Specific Regulation of Attorney Advertising: A Critique*, 18 U. Fla. J.L. & Pub. Pol'y 259, 259 (2007) (citing Fla. Bar v. Went For It, 515 U.S. 618, 620 (1995)).

In following Florida's lead, the LSBA Committee intentionally incorporated Florida's model of "aggressive regulation" of lawyer advertising.[24] Indeed, the LSBA purposely decided to regulate advertising to fullest extent constitutionally permissible and determined that Florida provided an excellent model for doing so.[25]

By October 27, 2006, the LSBA Committee had drafted proposed rules.[26] These rules retained the prior rules' over-arching prohibition on any false, misleading, or deceptive advertisement.[27] The proposal also added numerous more specific rules that would greatly restrict many types of lawyer advertising in Louisiana for the first time. The three most important proposed changes included: (1) new stringent restrictions on the contents of advertisements; (2) the creation of a new "safe-harbor" provision, which would make certain types of "plain vanilla"[28] advertisements presumptively in compliance with the rules;[29] and (3) the imposition of a new duty to file all advertisements outside of the safe harbor with the LSBA.[30] The filing requirement would apply to all advertisements, regardless of the medium of publication, including print, radio, television, and internet.[31]

Among the proposed content restrictions were complete prohibitions on certain content, including "any reference to past success or results obtained,"[32] testimonials,[33] depictions of the "use of a courtroom,"[34] "any background sound other than instrumental music,"[35] "non-authentic scenes,"[36] and "any spokesperson's voice or image that is recognizable to the public in the community where the advertisement appears."[37] At the other extreme, the rules created a "safe-harbor" provision, which made presumptively permissible any publication simply containing the lawyer's name, law firm, address, phone number, location, and date of admission to the Louisiana bar.[38] For all advertisements outside of this safe-harbor but not specifically banned, the committee proposed additional or more onerous *disclaimer* requirements.[39]

---

[24] Transcript of Lafayette Hearing at 90:14-18 (comments of Richard Lemmler). See also id. at 91:10-21 (statements of Sam Gregorio and Larry Shea) (indicating that the committee intended to regulate to the fullest extent constitutionally permissible).
[25] Transcript of Shreveport Hearing at 90:8-91:9 (comments of Richard Plattsmier); 91:19-21 (comments of Larry Shea).
[26] See Louisiana Proposed Rules of Prof'l Conduct (10-27-2006) (hereinafter "Proposed Rules").
[27] *Compare* Louisiana Rules of Prof'l Conduct Rule 7.1(a) (2006) *with* Louisiana Proposed Rules of Prof'l Conduct 7.1(b)(1) (Proposed 10-27-2006).
[28] Transcript of Shreveport Hearing at 73:8-14 (comments of Richard Lemmler).
[29] See Proposed Rule 7.8.
[30] See Proposed Rule 7.2, 7.7.
[31] See id.
[32] Proposed Louisiana Rule of Professional Conduct 7.2(b)(1)(B), Louisiana State Bar Association Rules of Professional Conduct Committee (10/27/2006).
[33] Proposed Rule 7.2(b)(1)(E).
[34] Proposed Rule 7.2(b)(1)(H).
[35] Proposed Rule 7.5(b)(1)(D).
[36] Proposed Rule 7.2(b)(1)(F).
[37] Proposed Rule 7.5(b)(1)(C).
[38] Proposed Rule 7.2(b)(1).
[39] See Proposed Rule 7.3(b) (requiring public print advertisements to include disclosure: "The hiring of a lawyer is an important decision that should not be based solely upon

Additionally, the committee proposed a new process by which the Louisiana State Bar would screen all print, television, radio, and internet advertisements that did not fall into the safe harbor.[40] This screening would occur, at the advertising lawyer's choice, either prior to or concurrent with the publication of those advertisements.[41] Any lawyer would have the option to submit her advertisement for an "advance written advisory opinion"[42] regarding compliance with the specific content rules discussed above, as well as the overarching prohibition on any "misleading or deceptive" advertisements.[43]

Although the advisory opinion regarding the advertisement would, like all ethics advisory opinions, be non-binding on the Disciplinary Committee,[44] early submission would at least provide evidence of a good faith attempt to comply with Section 7 of the Rules of Professional Conduct.[45] Filing for an advisory opinion would also fulfill the advertising lawyer's new duty to file each advertisement with the LSBA.[46] Any lawyer not seeking an advance advisory opinion would, upon dissemination of her advertisement, still be required to file a copy of it with the Bar Association's Committee for evaluation of compliance with the lawyer advertising rules.[47] Also, regardless of when the lawyer decided to file, the new rules required her to remit a $175 filing fee along with her submission.[48]

The Supreme Court Committee met, considered, and voted to endorse the LSBA's proposed amendments on October 23, 2006.[49] Then, the LSBA held four public hearings on the proposed rules and incorporated some of the suggestions gathered at these hearings.[50] On June 7, 2007, the Louisiana House of Delegates voted to accept the LSBA's proposal and recommended that that Louisiana Supreme Court incorporate the proposed rules into the Rules of Professional Conduct.[51] On July 3, 2008, the Louisiana Supreme Court adopted the rules, which would become effective on December 1, 2008.[52]

---

advertisements."); Proposed Rule 7.4(b)(2)(B)(ii) (requiring that any mailing to a prospective client include "ADVERTISEMENT" at the top and lower left of each page); Proposed Rule 7.6(c)(3) (requiring the subject line of any email communication to a prospective client to state "LEGAL ADVERTISEMENT").

[40] *See* Proposed Rule 7.2, 7.7.
[41] Proposed Rule 7.7.
[42] Proposed Rule 7.7(b).
[43] Proposed Rule 7.2(b)(1) (prohibiting "false, misleading, deceptive, or unfair" communication about the lawyer or the lawyer's services"); Proposed Rule 7.2(b)(2) (prohibiting any "misleading or deceptive" factual statements); Proposed Rule 7.2(c)(1) (prohibiting the use of illustrations or photographs that are "likely to deceive, mislead, or confuse the viewer").
[44] Transcript of New Orleans Hearing at 102:13-103:19 (comments of Richard Lemmler).
[45] *Id.*
[46] *Id.*
[47] *See id.*
[48] *See Public Citizen*, 642 F. Supp. 2d at 559 (describing procedural and regulatory background).
[49] *Public Citizen*, 642 F. Supp. 2d at 544, 559-60.
[50] *See* Transcripts of Baton Rouge, Lafayette, New Orleans, and Shreveport Hearings. *See also Public Citizen*, 642 F. Supp. 2d at 544.
[51] *Public Citizen*, 642 F. Supp. 2d at 544.
[52] *Id.*

II.   Challenging Reform

   A. *Public Citizen* Lawsuit

In the fall of 2008, the organization Public Citizen, Inc., together with Morris Bart, Scott Wolfe, Jr., and various other Louisiana lawyers, filed a federal lawsuit[53] to enjoin the enforcement of the new rules on First Amendment grounds (*"Public Citizen"*).[54] In response to this lawsuit, the Louisiana Supreme Court postponed the effective date of the Rules until April 1, 2009,[55] apparently to allow the LSBA to commission a survey on the attitude of consumers and lawyers toward lawyer advertising in Louisiana.[56] The LSBA completed the survey, and the Louisiana Supreme Court ordered that implementing the rules be deferred until October 1, 2009 "to allow the LSBA and the Court to further study certain Rules in light of the constitutional challenges that have been raised."[57]

On March 11, 2009, the Louisiana Supreme Court specifically asked the LSBA Committee to review several of the challenged rules.[58] Ultimately, in accordance with the LSBA Committee's recommendations, the Supreme Court modified the rules prohibiting celebrity spokespeople, non-authentic scenes, and actors playing clients, so as to permit those advertisements as long as accompanied by a special disclaimer.[59] Subject to these modifications, the Supreme Court ordered that the new rules would become effective October 1, 2009.[60]

In response to the Supreme Court's modifications, the plaintiffs amended their complaints to allege that Louisiana still lacked evidence that certain lawyer advertising techniques had been misleading in Louisiana and thus lacked sufficient evidence to restrict those methods of lawyer advertising.[61] Plaintiffs' amended complaints also alleged that the recent amendments to the soon-to-be-effective rules failed to cure the unconstitutional restrictions by substituting disclaimer requirements and other limitations[62] for outright prohibitions on certain types of

---

[53] *Id.*
[54] *See id.*
[55] *See* Supreme Court of Louisiana, *Order* (February 18, 2008).
[56] *See Public Citizen*, 642 F. Supp. 2d at 544. Up until this point, both the Supreme Court Committee and the LSBA Committee had reviewed at least one survey conducted in Florida to gauge the citizenry of Florida's views on public advertising. *See generally* Transcript of Lafayette Hearing at 9:11-11:11 (comments of Phelps Gay). Apparently, neither committee had relied on any Louisiana-specific information up until this point. Several members of the bar complained at the public hearings that this lack of Louisiana-specific evidence presented major First Amendment problems. *See* Transcript of New Orleans Hearing at 36:20-37:23 (e.g., comments of Morris Bart).
[57] Supreme Court of Louisiana, *Order* (February 12, 2009).
[58] *Public Citizen*, 642 F. Supp. 2d at 544-45.
[59] *See* Proposed Louisiana Rules of Prof'l Conduct Rule 7.2(b) (amended December 18, 2006), *available at* www.lsba.org (hereinafter "Amended Proposed Rules").
[60] Supreme Court of Louisiana, *Order* (June 30, 2009).
[61] *See* First Amended Complaint, Doc. Num. 69 (filed June 30, 2009), at 13, 15.
[62] *See, e.g.*, Proposed Rule 7.2(c)(1)(D) (post 12/18/2006) (prohibiting testimonials about past successes *unless provided upon request of a prospective customer*) (emphasis added).

advertising.⁶³ Lastly, the plaintiffs continued to challenge the filing and screening requirements in Rule 7.7 as unconstitutional burdens on protected speech.⁶⁴

B. First Amendment Landscape

The legal profession has, for over thirty years, struggled to balance often-competing concerns of maintaining traditional values of "professionalism" with a lawyer's right to engage in expression protected by the First Amendment. Beginning with *Bates v. State Bar of Arizona*,⁶⁵ the United States Supreme Court recognized that at least some First Amendment protections apply to a lawyer's print advertisements.⁶⁶ In doing so, the Court rejected the idea that notions of professional dignity could overcome the First Amendment's broad reach.⁶⁷ The Court explained that even paid advertisements valuably "inform the public of the availability, nature, and prices of products and services, and thus performs an indispensible role in the allocation of resources in a free enterprise system."⁶⁸ Accordingly, the Court held in *Bates* that the State Bar of Arizona may not constitutionally prevent an attorney's truthful print advertisement containing the availability of and terms of routine legal services.⁶⁹ Underscoring the narrow scope of its holding in *Bates*, the Court pointed out that "the special problems of advertising on the electronic broadcast media will warrant special consideration."⁷⁰

After *Bates*, the Court decided *Central Hudson Gas & Electric Corp. v. Public Service Commission of New York*,⁷¹ in which it enunciated the general test which is still used to evaluate regulation of commercial speech. Commercial speech is speech that is made to further the speaker's pecuniary gain.⁷² Under the three-part *Central Hudson* test, commercial speech may be regulated where: (1) the state articulates a substantial interest; (2) the regulation directly advances the state's asserted interest; and (3) the regulation is drawn narrowly to serve the state's interest.⁷³

In *In re R.M.J.*,⁷⁴ the Supreme Court applied its *Central Hudson* framework to attorney advertising for the first time. The Court invalidated a rule that prohibited a lawyer from publishing a newspaper advertisement which stated that the lawyer practiced "real estate" law, even where this was true.⁷⁵ In doing so, the Court held that states cannot "place an absolute prohibition on certain types of potentially misleading

---

⁶³ *See* Amended Complaint, Doc. Num. 66 (filed June 29, 2009) (as to Plaintiff Scott Wolfe, Jr.); First Amended Complaint, Doc. Num. 69 (filed June 30, 2009) (as to Plaintiffs Public Citizen, Inc., Morris Bart, and William Gee), at 3.
⁶⁴ *See id.*
⁶⁵ 433 U.S. 350 (1977).
⁶⁶ *Bates*, 433 U.S. at 383, 388.
⁶⁷ *Id.* at 364-65.
⁶⁸ *Id.* at 364.
⁶⁹ *Id.* at 384.
⁷⁰ *Id.* at 384.
⁷¹ 447 U.S. 557 (1980).
⁷² *See Ohralik v. Ohio State Bar Ass'n*, 436 U.S. 447, 454 (1978).
⁷³ *Central Hudson*, 447 U.S. at 563-64.
⁷⁴ 455 U.S. 191 (1982).
⁷⁵ *Id.* at 197.

information . . . if the information may also be presented in a way that is not deceptive."[76]

Today, the First Amendment analysis of a state's professional advertising restrictions has evolved into a two-step inquiry. First, the Court must consider whether the regulated information is "inherently misleading," in which case significant restrictions are permissible.[77] Although the First Amendment protects truthful relevant commercial information,[78] false, deceptive, or misleading advertising may clearly be restricted.[79] Indeed, a state may "freely regulate" (i.e., completely ban) commercial information that is "inherently likely to deceive"[80] or has been proven to be misleading.[81] Further, a state may prohibit any "particular form or method of advertising" that it can prove has actually been deceptive.[82]

Second, even if a court determines that the information is not inherently misleading, the court must consider whether the information has the potential to be deceptive. Information that is only "potentially misleading" may not be completely banned so long as it "may also be presented in a way that is not deceptive."[83] For information that is not categorically misleading but merely has the potential to be misleading, the court must apply the *Central Hudson* test. That is, a state may only regulate that speech where the state (1) articulates a substantial interest in regulating the speech, (2) narrowly draws the regulation, and (3) interferes with speech only in proportion to the interest served by the regulation.[84] In the commercial speech context, the state must merely demonstrate a "reasonable fit" between the state's interest and the means chosen to accomplish the ends; however, the regulation need not be the "least restrictive means" of advancing the state's interest.[85] In the case of potentially misleading speech, the Supreme Court has repeatedly upheld limited restrictions, including requirements that disclaimers or disclosures accompany certain types of information.[86]

---

[76] *Id.* at 203.
[77] *See Went For It, Inc.*, 515 U.S. at 623-24.
[78] *Ibanez v. Fla. Dep't of Bus. and Prof'l Regulation, Bd. of Accountancy*, 512 U.S. 136, 142 (1994) (holding that it is not misleading for an attorney/accountant to use designations of "CPA" and "CFP" on letterhead and advertisements as long as the designations are true).
[79] *In re R.M.J.*, 455 U.S. at 202-03 ("misleading advertising may be prohibited entirely"); *Ibanez*, 512 U.S. at 142 ("only false, deceptive, or misleading commercial speech may be banned").
[80] *Went For It*, 515 U.S. at 624.
[81] *Friedman v. Rogers*, 440 U.S. 1, 16 (1979) (upholding prophylactic prohibition on use of trade names by optometrists based upon actual experience which established possibilities for deception of the public).
[82] *In re R.M.J.*, 455 U.S. at 202.
[83] *Id.* at 203.
[84] *Id.* at 203 (citing *Central Hudson*). *See also The Florida Bar v. Herrick*, 571 So. 2d 1303, 1305 (Fla. 1990) (concluding that a state's rules on attorney advertising "may be no broader than reasonably necessary to prevent the perceived evil").
[85] *Went For It*, 515 U.S. at 632. This stands in contrast to political speech and strict scrutiny analysis, and is only true because of the lesser protection given commercial speech.
[86] *See In re R.M.J.*, 455 U.S. at 203 (indicating that certain disclosure language may be necessary to avoid potentially misleading the public); *Zauderer v. Office of Disciplinary Council*, 471 U.S. 626, 655-56 (1985) (holding that a state may not categorically prohibit the publication of truthful

Notably, despite its remark in *Bates* that "the special problems of advertising on the electronic broadcast media will warrant special consideration,"[87] the Supreme Court's jurisprudence about attorneys' First Amendment rights remains limited to cases involving print advertisement.[88] Notwithstanding urging by litigants and scholars to clarify the place of television and Internet advertising,[89] the Court has left these "special problems" of new media for the lower courts to resolve. It is against this landscape that the U.S. District Court for the Eastern District of Louisiana decided *Public Citizen*.

C. *Public Citizen* Decision

1. Television Advertising Restrictions Upheld

On August 3, 2009, Judge Martin Feldman upheld the majority of the revised proposed rules' limitations and disclosure requirements for television advertising. In particular, the plaintiffs had challenged: Rule 7.2(c)(1)(D) (prohibiting a "reference or testimonial to past successes or results obtained," except where provided upon request); Rule 7.2(c)(1)(E) (prohibiting communications that "promise results"); and Rule 7.2(c)(1)(J) (prohibiting a communication that "includes the portrayal of a judge or jury").[90] In upholding these restrictions, Judge Feldman relied heavily on the LSBA's Louisiana-specific survey, which was prompted by the filing of the lawsuit.[91] The court found that the survey results showed that testimonials to past results,[92] communications that promise results,[93] and portrayals of a judge or jury[94] were all "inherently misleading" lawyer advertising practices in Louisiana.[95] Relying on *In re R.M.J.*, the court found that Louisiana was justified in completely prohibiting these types of advertisements.[96]

---

illustrations in attorney advertisements); *Peel v. Attorney Registration & Disciplinary Commission*, 496 U.S. 91, 110 (1990) (holding that a state may not totally ban an attorney from advertising her nationally recognized specializations but that appropriate disclosure requirements may be required to avoid any potentially misleading implications). *But see Milavetz, Gallop & Milavetz, P.A. v. United States*, No. 08-1119, 2010 WL 757616, at *16 (U.S. March 8, 2010) (Scalia, J., concurring) (arguing that Court should revisit the premise on which *Zauderer* rests—that the First Amendment interest implicated by disclosure requirements are necessarily weaker than the interest implicated when restrictions actually suppress speech).
[87] *Bates*, 433 U.S. at 384.
[88] *See* Lidsky & Peterson, *Medium-Specific Regulation*, 18 U. Fla. J.L. & Pub. Pol'y at 284 n.142.
[89] *See id.*
[90] *Public Citizen*, 642 F. Supp. 2d at 545-47.
[91] *See id.* at 553-54.
[92] *Id.* at 553 n.5 (discussing LSBA findings that "eighty-three (83%) percent of the public interviewed . . . indicated that they 'disagreed' with the statement that 'client testimonials in lawyer advertising are completely truthful").
[93] *Id.* at 553-54 (finding that "the plain text of the Rule prohibits only communications that are inherently misleading").
[94] *Id.* at 554 (citing LSBA study results finding that "59% of the public felt those advertisements implied that Louisiana courts can be manipulated by the lawyers in the ads").
[95] *Id.* at 553-54.
[96] *Id.* at 553.

Additionally, the court said that even if the advertising practices in question were only potentially misleading (as opposed to inherently misleading), each of these restrictions still passed the *Central Hudson* test.[97] Applying *Central Hudson*, the court found that Louisiana had articulated a substantial interest in both "maintaining the standards of the legal profession and in protecting consumers from misleading or deceptive advertising."[98] Lastly, the court found a "reasonable fit" between these interests and each challenged Rule.[99]

2. Internet Advertising Restrictions Found Unconstitutional

a. *Content Requirements and Restrictions*

In addition to the unsuccessful challenges to television advertising rules, the plaintiffs challenged several new rules as they applied to internet advertisements.[100] First, plaintiffs successfully challenged the disclaimer and disclosure requirements as they applied to internet advertisements.[101] Challenged rules included Rule 7.2(a) (requiring that all communications include the name of at least one lawyer, as well as the location of one or more bona fide office locations of the lawyer who will actually perform the services) and Rule 7.2(c)(10) (requiring all written disclosures required elsewhere in the rules to be "both spoken aloud and written legibly").[102]

In rejecting the disclosure and disclaimer restrictions as they apply to internet advertisements, the court reasoned that:

> The defendants point to no empirical or anecdotal evidence relating to online attorney advertising. They have not shown that the State studied online advertising techniques or methods and then attempted to formulate a Rule that directly advanced the State's interests and was narrowly tailored with respect to Internet advertising. Instead, the State, through its high court, simply applied the same Rules as those developed for television, radio, and print ads to Internet advertising. This Court is persuaded that Internet advertising differs significantly from advertising in traditional media.[103]

Judge Feldman went on to cite *Reno v. American Civil Liberties Union*,[104] in which the Supreme Court had remarked that "the Internet is not as 'invasive' as radio or television" and commented that Internet communications "do not appear on one's computer screen unbidden."[105] Thus, because Louisiana had ignored the "uniqueness of the Internet as compared to other broadcast media" and had failed to gather Internet-specific evidence, the content-based restrictions on internet advertising had failed *Central Hudson*.[106]

---

[97] *Id.* at 554-57.
[98] *Id.* at 554-55.
[99] *Id.* at 555-57.
[100] *Id.* at 558.
[101] *Id.*
[102] *Id.*
[103] *Id.* at 558.
[104] 521 U.S. 844 (1997).
[105] *Public Citizen*, 521 U.S. at 559 (citation omitted).
[106] *Id.*

b. Filing Requirements

The plaintiffs also challenged the constitutionality of Rule 7.7, which required that all internet advertisements (aside from those encompassed by the safe-harbor) be filed with the LSBA, along with a $175 fee, either prior to or concurrently with their publication.[107] Again agreeing with the plaintiffs, the court found Rule 7.7 to be unconstitutional as it applied to Internet communications. In doing so, the court reasoned:

> Neither the LSBA Findings nor the defendants address the unique considerations with Internet advertising, specifically, the short length of ads and the multiple variations used, each of which would be required to be filed as a unique advertisement. As such, the application of Rule 7.7 to Internet advertising is not supported by sufficient evidence.[108]

Thus, like the content-based restrictions on internet advertisements, Rule 7.7 had failed to come within the ambit of *In re R.M.J.* and had also failed the *Central Hudson* test.[109]

Additionally, the court relied heavily on plaintiffs' example of the prohibitively expensive nature of the filing requirements as to "pay-per-click" internet advertisements.[110] A pay-per-click advertisement is one that appears in the margins or "banners" of a search engine, like Google, in which the advertiser pays the host only when the ad is actually clicked.[111] In that example, plaintiffs noted that they had run Google pay-per-click ads for three months at a total cost of $160.63.[112] For this cost, the Plaintiffs could run 12 ad variations, which would have required twelve separate filings with the LSBA.[113] Each Rule 7.7 filing would cost the firm $175.[114] Accordingly, Plaintiffs would have had to pay $1,200 in LSBA filing fees to run three months' worth of ads costing approximately $160.[115] The court found this to be unreasonable and thus unconstitutional.[116]

III. Internet Advertising in Louisiana and in Other States after *Public Citizen*

A. Content Regulations Regarding "Electronic Media" or "Computer-Accessed Communications"

Not only does *Public Citizen* call into question existing lawyer advertising regulations in other states like Florida that share Louisiana's model, but it also raises questions about the constitutionality of internet advertising restrictions in many other states.

---

[107] *Id. See also* Revised Proposed Rule 7.7 (requiring most advertisements to be filed for LSBA approval prior to or concurrently with the lawyer's first dissemination of the advertisement).
[108] *Public Citizen*, 521 U.S. at at 559.
[109] *See id.*
[110] *See id.*
[111] *See id.* at 558 n.14.
[112] *Id.*
[113] *Id.*
[114] *Id.*
[115] *Id.*
[116] *Id.*

1. Florida

As discussed earlier, Louisiana's scheme for both the content of Internet advertisements and the advertisement filing scheme were lifted directly from Florida's rules.[117] Accordingly, Florida's rule is clearly subject to attack for both of the reasons the Louisiana rule fell in *Public Citizen*. Absent the Florida bar's gathering of significant empirical or anecdotal evidence suggesting that certain internet advertising techniques are inherently or potentially misleading,[118] Florida's rule regulating the content of ads on the internet is obviously subject to attack for the same reason the Louisiana rule was rejected by the *Public Citizen* court. Even assuming that the Florida bar had gathered the internet-specific evidence, which all indications suggest it did not,[119] *Public Citizen* still indicates that this formulation fails to consider the "unique nature" of the internet as a medium, as required by *Central Hudson*.[120]

2. Arizona

Aside from Florida and Louisiana, Arizona is the only other state with a specific rule restricting the content of "electronic media" or "computer-accessed communications."[121] Still, the Arizona rule may certainly be called into question under *Public Citizen*. Arizona Rule 7.2(e) provides that "[a]dvertisements on the electronic media may contain the *same information* as permitted in advertisements in the *print media*."[122] The Arizona rule, by its very text, clearly does that which *Public Citizen* says it cannot do: it simply applies the restrictions created for one type of advertising (print) to another discrete advertising medium (the internet).[123] Thus, if challenged, Arizona's content-based advertising restrictions likely fail *Central Hudson* and run afoul of the First Amendment.

3. Other States

Less obviously but equally problematic, the supreme courts of several other states have determined that content restrictions for print or television advertisements

---

[117] Part I(B), above.

[118] *See Public Citizen*, 642 F. Supp. 2d at 559 (noting where a state fails to consider the separate issues, the evidence does not support the restriction for a unique media like the internet).

[119] It appears that the Louisiana survey was the exact same survey used in Florida. Initially, Louisiana attempted to rely on the Florida bar's findings. *Cf.* Transcript of New Orleans Hearing at 36:20-37:23 (comments of Morris Bart). Only after the *Public Citizen* suit was filed did Louisiana conduct an independent survey, which by all indications, replicated the Florida survey but was simply disseminated to lawyers and the citizenry of Louisiana. *Id.*

[120] *See Public Citizen*, 642 F. Supp. 2d at 559.

[121] *See* American Bar Association, *Differences Between State Advertising and Solicitation Rules and the ABA Model Rules of Professional Conduct* (March 12, 2010), at 59-60.

[122] Arizona Rule of Prof'l Conduct Rule 7.2(e) (emphasis added).

[123] *See Public Citizen*, 642 F. Supp. 2d at 558 ("They have not shown that the State ... attempted to formulate a Rule that directly advanced the State's interests and was narrowly tailored with respect to Internet advertising. Instead, the State, through its high court, simply applied the same Rules as those developed for print ads ... to Internet advertising.").

automatically apply to advertising on the internet.[124] In her comprehensive survey of attorney advertising rules for the internet, Professor Nia Monroe concluded in 2005:

> While a particular ethics rule may be worded broadly enough to cover Internet advertising or narrowly enough to exclude it, the rule in states likely will be construed to permit lawyer advertising on Web sites, *subject to the compliance requirements that apply to other ads.*[125]

Thus, if *Public Citizen* withstands further judicial scrutiny, a significant number of states likely run afoul of the First Amendment by doing that which *Public Citizen* says they cannot: "simply appl[ying] the same Rules as those developed for television, radio, and print ads to Internet advertising."[126]

B. Filing Requirements for Internet Advertisements

Although a comprehensive survey of content-based internet restrictions is beyond the scope of this research,[127] *Public Citizen* seriously questions the continued validity of filing schemes for internet advertisements in several other states. In *Public Citizen*, the court was concerned not with the duty to file, but with the $175 filing fee that Louisiana attached to this duty. Relying almost solely on plaintiffs' evidence that the Louisiana scheme may require them to pay filing costs that were as much as thirteen times the cost of the advertisement itself,[128] the *Public Citizen* court essentially found the filing fee to be unreasonable as it applied to internet advertisements. Thus, *Public Citizen* indicates that fee requirements that are unduly burdensome are unconstitutional, a ruling which may well prove to be persuasive as other states adopt such rules and courts review their constitutionality.

1. States with De Minimus Burdens

At least nineteen other states impose some filing requirement upon lawyers who advertise in the state,[129] and as discussed in Part III(A)(3), most states have

---

[124] *See, e.g.*, J.T. Westermeier, *Ethics and the Internet*, 17 Geo. J. Legal Ethics 267, 275 (2004) (discussing Texas).
[125] Nia Marie Monroe, *The Need For Uniformity: Fifty Separate Voices Lead to Disunion in Attorney Internet Advertising*, 18 Geo. J. Legal Ethics 1005, 1013 (2005) (emphasis added).
[126] *See Public Citizen*, 642 F. Supp. 2d at 559.
[127] For a discussion of the near impossibility of reconciling internet regulations across the 50 states, *see* Monroe, *The Need For Uniformity*, 18 Geo. J. Legal Ethics at 1015.
[128] *See Public Citizen*, 642 F. Supp. 2d at 559 ("[Plaintiffs] ran pay-per-click ads during the months of April, May, and June, spending a total of $160.63 with Google (the 'leader' in such advertising). They ran approximately 12 ad variations, which would have required 12 separate filings with the LSBA, and would have cost [plaintiffs] approximately $2,100.").
[129] *See* Alabama Rules of Prof'l Conduct Rule 7.2(b); Arizona Rules of Prof'l Conduct Rule 7.3(c)(1); California Rules of Prof'l Conduct Rule 1-400(F); Connecticut Rules of Prof'l Conduct Rule 7.2; Connecticut Practice Book § 2-28(A)-(B); Florida Rules of Prof'l Conduct Rule 4-7.7(a)-(d); Hawaii Rules of Prof'l Conduct 7.3(c)(2); Indiana Rules of Prof'l Conduct Rule 7.3(c); Iowa Rules of Prof'l Conduct Rule 32:7.3(b); Kentucky Supr. Court Rule 3.130 (7.05-7.07); Mississippi Rule 7.5(a); Nevada Rule 7.2(b)-(c) and 7.2A; New York Rules of Prof'l Conduct Rule 7.3(c)(1), (2), (4) & (5); Rhode Island Rules of Prof'l Conduct Rule 7.2(b); South Carolina Rules of Prof'l Conduct Rule 7.2(b); South Dakota Rules of Prof'l Conduct Rule 7.3(c); Tennessee Rules of Prof'l Conduct Rule 7.2(b); Texas Rules of Prof'l Conduct 7.07(a);

determined that the requirements for television and radio advertisements also apply to internet advertising. Many states avoid the problems identified in *Public Citizen* by merely requiring a lawyer to mail (or even email) a copy of her advertisement to the state bar or its disciplinary board within a specified time period. Alabama,[130] Connecticut, Nevada,[131] Rhode Island,[132] and Virginia[133] follow this formulation. Many more states have "filing" requirements that simply require the lawyer to maintain a copy of the advertisement or changes to a website in her own records for a specified time period.[134] None of these states assesses any fee, other than potentially postage fees for mailing a hard copy of the advertisement to the state. Thus, these formulations appear to avoid First Amendment problems by imposing a *de minimus* burden on lawyers who advertise in their states.

2. South Carolina, Kentucky, and Texas

In contrast to the *de minimus* filing requirements discussed in Part III(B)(1), this author has identified four states that impose requirements that are likely to raise First Amendment issues after *Public Citizen*. South Carolina, Kentucky, and Texas have filing rules which both assess fees and are likely broad enough to encompass internet advertisements. South Carolina Rule 7.2(b) requires that a copy of every advertisement

> shall be filed with the Commission on Lawyer Conduct within ten (10) days after the advertisement is first published, broadcast, *transmitted, or otherwise disseminated* to the public, together with a fee of $50.00.[135]

Similarly, Kentucky requires the submission of any advertisement published by "any broadcast media," together with a "filing fee of $50.00 for each advertisement filed."[136] Texas requires a lawyer to file any "electronic, written, audio, audio-visual, digital or other electronic solicitation communication," together with "the fee set by the Board of Directors."[137] This fee is currently $75.00.[138]

Applying the "pay-per-click" example in *Public Citizen*, each of the filing requirements above is likely too burdensome to pass First Amendment scrutiny. Using the *Public Citizen* plaintiffs' "pay-per-click" example, an attorney would have to pay fees of $600 in South Carolina and Kentucky and $900 in Texas to run an advertisement that

---

Virginia Rules of Prof'l Conduct Rule 7.2(b); Wisconsin Rules of Prof'l Conduct Rule 20:7.3(c). *See also* American Bar Association, *Differences Between State Advertising and Solicitation Rules and the ABA Model Rules of Professional Conduct* (March 12, 2010), at 33-50.

[130] *See* Alabama Rules of Prof'l Conduct Rule 7.3(b)(2)(i).
[131] *See* Nevada Rules of Prof'l Conduct Rule 7.2(j).
[132] *See* Rhode Island Rules of Prof'l Conduct Rule 7.2(b).
[133] *See* Virginia Rules of Prof'l Conduct Rule 7.2(b).
[134] *See, e.g.*, Connecticut Rules of Prof'l Conduct Rule 7.2; Connecticut Practice Book § 2-28(A)-(B).
[135] South Carolina R. Prof'l Conduct Rule 7.2(b) (emphasis added).
[136] *See* Kentucky Supreme Court Rule 3.130(1)(b), (2).
[137] *See* Texas Rules of Prof'l Conduct Rule 7.07(a).
[138] State Bar of Texas, *Frequently Asked Questions* (last visited March 23, 2010), *available at* http://www.texasbar.com/Content/ContentGroupsl/Professional_Requirementsl/Advertising_Reviewl/FAQsl/Frequently_Asked_Questions.htm.

itself costs only $160. To be sure, the Supreme Court has indicated that, in some instances, a licensing fee designed to defray the administrative costs associated with state supervision is permissible;[139] however, the Supreme Court has never addressed the fee issue as it relates to internet advertising. The *Public Citizen* court did not address this particular issue and precedent either. Although it remains to be seen whether "administrative costs" that double, triple, or amount to thirteen times the cost of an advertisement itself can be justified as "defraying the cost of administration," this author suggests that such mounting costs are unreasonable and thus constitute unconstitutional burdens on speech. Accordingly, the burdensome, bureaucratic filing systems discussed above may simply be incompatible with the fast-paced and inexpensive nature of internet advertising, at least as long as states assess fees to attorney-advertisers to fund their regulatory regimes.

3. Mississippi

Mississippi provides one possible solution to the problem identified in Part III(B)(2), as Mississippi purports to exempt internet information from the filing and filing fee requirements.[140] Exempt from its filing requirement are "Internet Web pages viewed via a Web browser, in a search initiated by a person *without solicitation*."[141] Despite the broad wording of this exemption, it seems that a "pay-per-click" advertisement would still fall outside of the exemption. Although one could argue that clicking on the hyperlink within the pay-per-click ad constitutes a new search "initiated by" the user, the appearance of the advertisement itself on a web banner is arguably solicitation in this sense, as it is currently understood.[142]

Pay-per-click advertisements appear in the margins ("the banner") of the user's search engine based on her previous searches.[143] Like the recipient of a targeted mailing or a television commercial, the recipient of a pay-per-click advertisement receives the ad based on an outside actor's determination that this is the type of individual who is likely to need the lawyer's services. While traditional solicitation may be based on market research compiled by the lawyer or a marketing firm, pay-per-click ad recipients are determined when one's own browser instantly compiles information about the user based on her past searches. The method by which this information is gathered does not alter the fact that its goal is to seek potential business for a lawyer. Therefore, the Mississippi example illustrates that the problems raised in *Public Citizen* are not easily cured, even with seemingly broad exemptions from filing for internet publications.

---

[139] Cox v. New Hampshire, 312 U.S. 569, 577 (1941) (finding licensing fee of $300 designed to defray the administrative costs associated with the supervision of parades was justified). *See also* Texans Against Censorship v. State Bar of Texas, 888 F. Supp. 1328, 1365 (E.D. Tex. 1995) (citing *Cox*, but not reaching the issue of whether the filing fee was unduly burdensome).
[140] *See* Mississippi Rules of Prof'l Conduct Rule 7.5(b)(8) (exempting from filing any "Internet Web pages viewed via a Web browser, in a search initiated by a person without solicitation"); Mississippi Rule of Prof'l Conduct Rule 7.5(c)(4) (discussing fee).
[141] Mississippi Rules of Prof'l Conduct Rule 7.5(b)(8) (emphasis added).
[142] *See Ohralik*, 436 U.S. at 454 (discussing key elements of solicitation as "seeking employment for pecuniary gain").
[143] *See Public Citizen*, 642 F. Supp. 2d at 558 n.14 (discussing pay-per-click advertisements).

IV. Conclusion

Legal scholars have repeatedly noted that Supreme Court jurisprudence on lawyer advertising remains limited to print advertisements[144] — and have criticized the High Court's repeated inattention,[145] or refusal[146] depending on one's perspective, to examine lawyer advertising restrictions beyond those that apply to traditional print media or in-person solicitation. Against this backdrop, states have largely ignored the Court's admonishment in *Bates* to specially consider new technology. Instead, states have assumed that they may constitutionally limit attorney advertising on the internet to the fullest extent that television and print advertising may be regulated.

Public Citizen challenges this basic assumption that internet advertising is sufficiently analogous to the print and television advertising. In doing so, it also challenges the assumption that a state may apply to the internet a filing regime that was developed for, and has been upheld as to, television and print. A review of the filing schemes in other states supports the conclusion in *Public Citizen* that filing and review mechanisms created for television and print advertisements are too burdensome when applied to inexpensive and efficient internet advertisement technology. Further, the problems with even a broadly worded exemption like Mississippi's indicate that filing schemes developed to screen television advertisements may simply be incompatible with internet advertising.

In light of the Louisiana experience, other state supreme courts and bar organizations should promptly review and assess their own regulations of internet advertising by lawyers. This is so even as to implicit regulations that have not been exempted from more general requirements, procedures, and fees.

In particular, South Carolina, Kentucky, Texas, and Mississippi should carefully review the filing requirements that they currently apply to internet advertising. In doing so, they should seriously consider the possibility that slow-moving, expensive, and bureaucratic filing and review schemes are simply incompatible with fast-paced and inexpensive internet advertising. If these states fail to do so, they risk defending expensive and protracted First Amendment litigation which, like *Public Citizen*, may ultimately invalidate their own regulations.

---

[144] *See, e.g.*, Lidsky & Peterson, *Medium-Specific Regulation*, 18 U. Fla. J.L. & Pub. Pol'y at 284 n.142 (noting that in both *Bates* and *Zauderer*, the Court expressly limited its holding to advertisements of routine legal services in print).

[145] *See* Ralph H. Brock, *"The Court Took a Wrong Turn With Bates": Why the Supreme Court Should Revisit Lawyer Advertising*, 7 First Amend. L. Rev. 145, 164 (2009).

[146] *See* Lidsky & Peterson, 18 U. Fla. J.L. & Pub. Pol'y at 284 n.142.

Chapter 2

"Friends," Episode 1: The Ethical Pitfalls of Lawyers Getting "Friendly" Online

Lara K. Richards

Facebook, MySpace, LinkedIn, Twitter. Five years ago, these words were foreign concepts in the legal realm. Nowadays, having an online presence is a key ingredient to running a successful law practice. Law firms not only have web pages, but many lawyers operate blogs about their practice areas. Countless lawyers also maintain more personal profiles on social networking sites such as Facebook and MySpace in an attempt to market themselves to technology-savvy consumers. Attracting the modern-day client means embracing new technology to stay on the cutting edge.

Using the Internet is not just an effective marketing tool for lawyers; it is also a treasure trove of information for lawyers seeking information to aid their cases. Lawyers now routinely "Google" opposing counsel, witnesses, and even judges to mine web sites for useful information to prepare for litigation. Selecting jurors during voir dire means first conducting an extensive online search through police records, public records, newspaper clippings, campaign contributions sheets, and other Internet-accessible documents. Doing a thorough investigation of an opposing party's witness means scouring the Internet for information.

The use of technology in the legal practice has progressed faster than the American Bar Association's Model Rules of Professional Conduct have kept up, and lawyers and legal analysts are attempting to define the parameters of the increasing use of technology in the profession.[147] The lack of guidance from the Model Rules is especially troubling and confusing in terms of the appropriate uses of social networking in the legal industry.[148] The Model Rules were written in a world where most communications took place either on the phone or in person. The idea of trolling the Internet for data for a case, contacting someone by email or BlackBerry, or leaving messages for people on their Facebook page was unimaginable then. In today's technological world, though, it is vitally important that lawyers know the parameters for their use of social networking.

For example, to what extent can an attorney, or those working for him, search the Internet for information about a future witness or juror? What kind of information-seeking techniques would count as deceptive practices under Rule 8.4 – using a screen name instead of one's real name online? Does "friending" someone online with

---

[147] *See, e.g.*, Judy M. Cornett, *The Ethics of Blawging: A Genre Analysis*, 41 Loy. U. Chi. L.J. 221 (2009); Adam R. Bialek et.al., *Attorney Web Sites: Ethical Issues Are Only the Beginning*, 81 N.Y. St. B.J. 10 (2009).

[148] Steven C. Bennett, *Ethics of Lawyer Social Networking*, 73 Alb. L. Rev. 113, 114 (2009) ("[Social networking] and the frequency of its use has already outpaced established legal practices. Existing ethics guidelines generally do not focus on technology issues, and state bar associations have been slow to fill in the gaps with opinions and best practice guides.").

the sole purpose of accessing their MySpace page for use in litigation constitute a violation of Rule 4.1, which demands truthfulness in statements to others? *Do the current Model Rules cover social networking at all?*

Part I of this paper will discuss the way that social networking has changed the way that lawyers conduct their practices. Part II will analyze the ethical pitfalls inherent in utilizing social networking as a lawyer. In it, I discuss two recent ethics opinions concerning "friending" on Facebook, and a judicial reprimand of one North Carolina judge concerning his online "friendship" with a lawyer. Part III will explore the ethical gray areas left unexamined – or perhaps created – by these two ethics opinions, analyzing the difficulty of applying the current Model Rules of Professional Conduct to online relationships and investigations conducted through social networking sites. Part IV will conclude with an analysis of what I view are the two biggest problems with the current consensus on lawyers' ethical obligations regarding social networking.

I. Social Networking and Lawyers

Open up any bar journal publication or legal magazine today and you'll find numerous articles discussing lawyers and social networking.[149] This facet of the Internet has exploded in recent years as lawyers explore social networking avenues for ways to show their expertise, grow their exposure, and attract new clients.[150] While some practitioners lament that the Internet is a poor substitute for face-to-face cultivation of relationships with clients, newer generation lawyers have turned to social networking as a "brilliant way to connect with people."[151] For beginning lawyers who a struggling to build a practice and establish a clientele, having a strong online presence is touted as a key resource to gaining needed exposure.[152] As the next generation of lawyers, which have grown up with the Internet, become bosses and business owners, the use of social networking is only expected to increase in the legal industry.[153]

While lawyers are embracing the power of the Internet as a marketing tool, going online is also a very cheap and easy way for attorneys to research opposing counsel, judges, witnesses, and even potential jurors in a case.[154] A simple Google search can

---

[149] *See, e.g.,* Kelly Phillips Erb, *Put Your Best Face Forward – Online*, 31 Pa. Law 32 (2009) (discussing how social networking can be a powerful marketing tool for today's lawyers).

[150] Doug Cornelius, *Online Networking for Lawyers*, 45 TRIAL 20 (2009); *see also* Daniel E. Harmon, *Notes on More "Sociable" Networking, Passionate Blogging and Diligent Doctoring*, 27 No. 8 Law. PC 7 (2010) ("Social networking sites are excellent venues for cultivating—and multiplying—client friendships.").

[151] Daniel E. Harmon, *"Let's Just Be Friends": Leverage Social Network Platforms by Simply "Being There,"* 27 No. 9 Law. PC 1 (2010).

[152] *See* Clare D. Membiela, *Sources to Help New Attorneys "Bridge the Gap" Instead of Step In It*, 88 Mich. B.J. 56 (2009); Denise Howell & Ernie Svenson, *Ins and Outs of Social Networking for Lawyers: How Tough Is It to Cast Your Profile into Infinity*, 34 Law Prac. 47 (2008).

[153] Liz McKenzie, *Poking Around Facebook Could Win Your Case*, Feb. 4, 2010, http:www.law360.com/articles/147130.

[154] *See, e.g.,* Jeffrey T. Frederick, *You, the Jury, and the Internet*, 39 WTR Brief 12 (2010) (arguing that online investigations can lead to more effective questioning of jurors during voir dire).

immediately pull up a variety of web sites in which someone is listed, from newspaper articles to business listings to even using Google Streetview to see the front of the person's home.[155] Lawyers can also search for campaign contributions, workers' compensation claims, arrest records, and even lawsuit filings to get a more complete picture of a future witness or potential juror.[156]

Social networking sites such as MySpace and Facebook, however, often possess an added level of information for lawyers because of their semi-private nature.[157] To view someone's Facebook page, one must be "friended" or given access by the page moderator to see the page's contents.[158] As a result, Facebook and MySpace users often expose a greater level of detail about their lives on these pages versus their non-protected blogs and other web sites that do not require permission to view – details that can prove very useful to lawyers.[159] These social networking sites have been labeled a "powerful game-changer for attorneys" and a "goldmine of info" to access during litigation as these sites feature photos, detailed descriptions of events, and even lists of friends that could be potential witnesses or interview subjects.[160]

There are countless stories about how a posting on a social networking site proved to be the smoking gun in cases ranging from personal injury to sexual harassment to divorce and child custody litigation.[161] For instance, one worker's product liability suit was dismissed after defense lawyers found photos of the man on Facebook racing motorboats, even though the man had filed disability claims for years.[162] A woman who was charged with driving under the influence, which resulted in the death of a passenger, had hoped for probation from the judge at her sentencing hearing. But when the prosecution showed photos from her MySpace page showing her wearing a liquor company's T-shirt and partying with friends, the judge was doubtful she had remorse for her crime and sentenced her to five years and four months in prison.[163]

Divorce attorneys have repeatedly found ample ammunition for their cases on social networking sites, especially proof of infidelity.[164] Family court attorneys also troll the

---

[155] See Christopher B. Hopkins, *Internet Social Networking Sites for Lawyers*, 28 No. 2 Trial Advoc. Q. 12, 13 (2009).

[156] *Id.* at 13-14.

[157] John G. Browning, *What Lawyers Need to Know About Social Networking Sites*, Feb. 1, 2009, http://www.dallasbar.org/about/news-archives.asp?ID=240 (noting that "social networking can be an important weapon in any lawyer's arsenal").

[158] *See* Hopkins, *Internet Social Networking*, 28 No. 2 Trial Advoc. Q. 12 (2009).

[159] McKenzie, *Poking Around Facebook*, Feb. 4, 2010, http:www.law360.com/articles/147130.

[160] *Id.*

[161] Leora Maccabee, *Facebook 101: Why Lawyers Should Be on Facebook*, April 23, 2009, www.lawyerist.com/facebook-101-why-lawyers-should-be-on-facebook/ ("Facebook can be an effective tool for investigating defendants, witnesses, and prosecutors. Evidence revealed from profile searches has been used to prove that a defendant has no remorse after committing a crime, to prove a defendant's motive,...and to show the extent of plaintiffs' injuries after an accident.").

[162] *Id.*

[163] Browning, *What Lawyers Need to Know*, Feb. 1, 2009, http://www.dallasbar.org/about/news-archives.asp?ID=240.

[164] Larry Hartstein, *Facebook a Treasure Trove for Divorce Lawyers*, Atlanta J. Const., Feb. 11, 2010, www.ajc.com/news/facebook-a-treasure-trove-298403.html ("A good attorney can have a field

sites for information about the fitness of the parents in custody cases, often finding damaging postings by parents, such as one mother who told the court she had quit drinking, but had posted actual dated photos of her drinking and smoking on her MySpace page.[165] As one bar association recently noted, "Simply put, evidence from social networking sites is being used in all kinds of cases. Few things undermine a sexual harassment plaintiff's claims of innocence faster than revealing that the plaintiff has a MySpace page that looks like a 'Girls Gone Wild' video."[166]

The information gleaned from social networking sites is increasingly used as evidence in court.[167] Lawyers routinely subpoena information from Facebook when they file suits as part of the discovery process.[168] As a result, one of the first things a good defense lawyer will make the client do is delete his or her social networking profiles.[169] To combat the destruction of pages, both Facebook and MySpace have established protocols in place whereby attorneys can request that the companies preserve pages for use in litigation.[170]

It is no surprise, then, that attorneys "love these (social networking) sites, which can be evidentiary gold mines."[171] Yet the question remains: what tools may lawyers use to mine for this litigation gold?[172]

II. Ethical Landmines for Lawyers

As noted, social networking sites contain an intimate look inside a person's private life, which can prove highly advantageous for lawyers during litigation. "Social networking sites can provide a wealth of information for lawyers. From education background to work history to intimate revelations and incriminating video, this

---

day with this information."); Dareh Gregorian, *Facebook 'Em!—Online Evidence Nailing Stray Spouses*, N.Y. Post, Feb. 11, 2010, at 15 (noting that 81 percent of matrimonial lawyers had said they had seen a massive spike in the use of social networking information as evidence of infidelity).

[165] Belinda Luscombe, *Facebook and Divorce: Airing the Dirty Laundry*, Time, June 22, 2009, http://www.time.com/time/magazine/article/0,9171,1904147,00.html ("Battles over finances and custody remain the Iwo Jima and Stalingrad of divorce cases. Opposing lawyers will press any advantage they have, and personal information [on social networking sites] is like decoded bulletins from enemy territory.").

[166] *Quoted in* Browning, *What Lawyers Need to Know*, Feb. 1, 2009, http://www.dallasbar.org/about/news-archives.asp?ID=240.

[167] McKenzie, *Poking Around Facebook*, Feb. 4, 2010, http:www.law360.com/articles/147130.

[168] *Id.*

[169] Brian Malcom, *Web 2.0--Lawyer to Client: Delete Your Facebook Profile*, Young Lawyers Blog, Feb. 16, 2010, http://www.younglawyersblog.com/post/Web-20-Lawyer-to-Client-Delete-Your-Facebook-Profile.aspx.

[170] Hopkins, *Internet Social Networking*, 28 No. 2 Trial Advoc. Q. 12, 15 (2009).

[171] Luscombe, *Facebook and Divorce*, Time, June 22, 2009.

[172] Lawyers have expressed concern about the ethical uncertainty of using social networking in their practices. *See* Helen Gunnarsson, *Social Media and Legal Ethics*, 97 Ill. B.J. 438 (2009) ("Perhaps you're tempted to try Twitter, or Facebook, or LinkedIn, as other lawyers are doing in droves, but haven't yet done so in part out of fear that you may unwittingly commit an ethical blunder using unfamiliar social networking media. What's the conscientious 21st century lawyer to do?").

digital treasure trove is [a lawyer's] for the taking when access is unlimited."[173] But *what about when access is limited?* What steps may an attorney, or those working for her, take to access information that is barred from viewing by the general public?

The problem with mining Facebook and MySpace pages for data is that getting access to view these pages requires that the person who created the page grant the prospective viewer access. The Model Rules do not directly address the issue of the permissible means that a lawyer may use to gain access to a potential juror or witnesses' private social networking sites. Nevertheless, two recent ethics advisory opinions in Florida and Pennsylvania, as well as a judicial reprimand in North Carolina, shed light on the ethical expectations for lawyers and judges when using social networking sites.

A. Philadelphia Bar Association Ethics Opinion

The issue of accessing social networking sites to dig for information about a witness was recently the subject of an ethics advisory inquiry from a Philadelphia lawyer.[174] In one of that lawyer's cases, a witness for the opposing party revealed during a deposition that she had both Facebook and MySpace accounts. During the deposition, the attorney did not ask the witness about the contents of her page, nor did he ask for access to them. After the deposition, however, he and his assistant visited both social networking sites and attempted to access the witness's accounts. It was then that the attorney discovered that he could only obtain permission from the witness herself to view the pages.

The attorney subsequently inquired with the Philadelphia Bar Association's Professional Guidance Committee whether it would be permissible for him to ask a third person, such as his paralegal, to contact the witness and seek to "friend" her so that the witness would grant access to the restricted pages. The paralegal would only state truthful information, such as his real name, but would not reveal that he was affiliated with the law firm. The paralegal would also not reveal that the true reason for seeking "friendship" status would be to acquire information from the MySpace and Facebook pages that the lawyer could use in the pending litigation.[175]

The ethics advisory opinion from the Philadelphia Bar noted that several ethical issues were raised by the lawyer's hypothetical question. First, if the attorney directed a subordinate – either a paralegal, a law clerk, or even an investigator – to access the site, then the lawyer would be held responsible for the nonlawyer assistants' conduct under Rule 5.3.[176] Second, regardless of who accessed the site, the Committee stated that the action would violate Rule 8.4(c) because the planned communication would be deceptive.[177] The Committee noted that the only reason the third party would ask for access to the witness's pages would be to obtain

---

[173] Browning, *What Lawyers Need to Know*, Feb. 1, 2009, http://www.dallasbar.org/about/news-archives.asp?ID=240.
[174] Philadelphia Bar Ass'n Professional Guidance Committee Op. 2009-02 (2009), *available at* http://www.philadelphiabar.org/WebObjects/PBAReadOnly.woa/Contents/WebServerResources/CMSResources/Opinion_2009-2.pdf [hereinafter Philadelphia Opinion].
[175] *Id.*
[176] *Id.* at *2.
[177] *Id.* at *2-3.

information and then share it with the lawyer.¹⁷⁸ Therefore, the "friending" would be occurring under false pretenses. Third, the Committee noted that the proposed course of conduct would also violate Rule 4.1, which dictates that a lawyer shall not make false statements to others.¹⁷⁹

The attorney attempted to justify his proposed course of conduct by arguing that it was possible that the witness was a very liberal "friender" and that she would let most anyone view her site without doing much of an investigation prior to granting access.¹⁸⁰ The Committee, however, said that the witness's conduct when granting access to her site was irrelevant.¹⁸¹ The opinion stated, "Deception is deception, regardless of the victim's wariness in her interactions on the internet and susceptibility to being deceived. The fact that access to the pages may be readily obtained by others who either are or are not deceiving the witness . . . does not mean that deception at the direction of the [inquiring attorney] is ethical."¹⁸² The Committee stated that the proposed plan to gain access to the witness's Facebook and MySpace pages would be a violation of the applicable state version of the ABA Model Rules, and should not be pursued.

B. Florida Ethics Advisory Opinion

The Florida Supreme Court Judicial Ethics Advisory Committee also recently issued an advisory opinion regarding judges' actions on social networking sites.¹⁸³ A judge in that state had inquired whether judges might "friend" lawyers who might appear before him in court, and vice versa. The Committee analyzed the issue under the state of Florida's Code of Judicial Conduct, specifically Canon 2B, which states that a judge is prohibited from appearing as if he is advancing the interests of another or that he permits others to give the impression that they have special favor with that judge.¹⁸⁴ The Committee wrote that judges' "friending" lawyers violates that canon because it "reasonably conveys to others the impression that these lawyer 'friends' are in a special position to influence the judge."¹⁸⁵ The opinion noted that it was not recommending that a judge refrain from social networking completely or "friending" in general; the judge would still be permitted to "friend" people not in the legal profession or lawyers that would never appear before that judge.¹⁸⁶

---

[178] *Id.* at *3.
[179] *Id.* at *4.
[180] *Id.* at *1.
[181] *Id.* at *3.
[182] *Id.* at *3.
[183] Florida Supreme Court Judicial Ethics Advisory Committee Op. 2009-20 (2009), *available at* http://www.jud6.org/LegalCommunity/LegalPractice/opinions/jeacopinions/2009/2009-20.html [hereinafter Florida Opinion].
[184] *Id.* Canon 2, subsection B reads: "A judge shall not lend the prestige of judicial office to advance the private interests of the judge or others; nor shall a judge convey or permit others to convey the impression that they are in special position to influence the judge."
[185] Florida Opinion, *available at* http://www.jud6.org/LegalCommunity/LegalPractice/opinions/jeacopinions/2009/2009-20.html .
[186] *Id.*

A minority group of members on the Committee, however, would have permitted the judge to "friend" lawyers appearing before him, and lawyers to friend the judge.[187] The minority noted that "friending" does not connote a special relationship with a judge because people that utilize social networking sites routinely "friend" people that they are not actually friends with in the real world. The minority wrote "that social networking sites have become so ubiquitous that the term 'friend' on these pages does not convey the same meaning that it did in the pre-internet age; that today, the term 'friend' on social networking sites merely conveys the message that a person so identified is a contact or acquaintance."[188] The minority members believed that being labeled a "friend" on the Internet does not mean that a judge is a friend with someone in the traditional sense, and that frequent users of these types of sites are aware of the level of informality of these "friendly" relationships. As such, being "friends" on Facebook, MySpace, and other social networking sites with an attorney that came before a judge in court would not violate the Judicial Code of Conduct, according to the minority of the Committee.[189]

C. Public Reprimand of B. Carlton Terry, Jr.

A North Carolina judge was recently reprimanded by the Judicial Standards Commission in North Carolina for friending a lawyer during litigation.[190] Judge B. Carlton Terry, Jr., was presiding over a child custody and child support hearing when one of the attorneys in the case spoke about Facebook while in the judge's chambers. After the conversation, Judge Terry and the lawyer for the defendant in the case "friended" each other on Facebook.[191] They subsequently exchanged a few postings with each other about the case on their pages. For instance, the lawyer once posted, "I have a wise Judge."[192] In addition, the lawyer also posted, "I hope I'm in my last day of trial," to which Judge Terry weighed in, "you are in your last day of trial."[193]

The North Carolina disciplinary board, unsurprisingly, ruled that Judge Terry's postings on Facebook with the lawyer constituted ex parte communications which were prohibited under the North Carolina Code of Judicial Conduct.[194] The board wrote that Judge Terry had failed "to act at all times in a manner that promotes public confidence in the integrity and impartiality of the judiciary."[195] The Commission publicly reprimanded the judge for his actions.[196]

---

[187] *Id.*

[188] *Id.*

[189] *Id.*

[190] Public Reprimand, B. Carlton Terry, Jr., North Carolina Judicial Standards Commission, Inquiry No. 08-234 (2009), *available at* http://www.aoc.state.nc.us/www/public/coa/jsc/publicreprimands/jsc08-234.pdf [*hereinafter* North Carolina Reprimand].

[191] *Id.* at *2.

[192] *Id.*

[193] *Id.*

[194] *Id.* at *3.

[195] *Id.* at *4. Judge Terry also committed another online misstep during the trial. He Googled the plaintiff to find out more information about her photography business. He visited her business's web site, viewing various photographs she had taken. He also read poems that she had posted online, and he subsequently quoted one of the poems when he announced his

Although Judge Terry's reprimand certainly presents an example of the dangers of online networking during a case, and a cautionary tale to be sure, it should be noted that the judge's conduct may well have been wrong regardless of the medium of communication he chose, rather than the use of the Internet or "friending" as such, outside of an ongoing case. It is not clear to what degree the opinion and its result indict more generally the concept of social networking.

III. Ethical Gray Areas in Social Networking

In the wake of the three recent ethical board decisions discussed above, numerous bar associations have weighed in on the issue of lawyers and judges using social networking. The discussions center on two main questions: (1) may attorneys or their subordinates gain access to someone's social networking site for purposes of gathering information for litigation without identifying their true purpose?; and (2) what exactly does it mean to be a "friend" someone on a social networking site? Determining the answers to these questions is a key to establishing what constitutes ethical conduct by lawyers on social networking sites.

A. Deception or Just Good Investigative Techniques?

Social networking sites are a valuable asset for lawyers during litigation as they may hold vital information – even ammunition – for a case. As lawyers have noted, "Courts have continued to hold that virtually anything posted online is fair game in court and can be used in discovery."[197] As such, it becomes increasingly important that lawyers are aware of the permissible – and most importantly impermissible – methods for obtaining the information they seek from these sites.[198] One key issue "related to the ever-expanding universe of modern technologies is whether attorneys may use misleading means to gain access to someone's social networking website."[199] The Philadelphia opinion called this action "deception," which would be a violation of the code of ethics; however, this is merely a non-binding advisory opinion from one city's bar association.

---

findings in the case. When the judge disclosed his Facebook activities, as well as his Googling of the plaintiff, to attorneys for both parties in the case, the plaintiff's attorney filed a motion in the case to vacate his orders. The judge subsequently disqualified himself from the case and a new trial was ordered. *Id.* at *2-3.

[196] *Id.* at *4-5.

[197] Liz McKenzie, *Poking Around Facebook Could Win Your Case*, Feb. 4, 2010, http:www.law360.com/articles/147130.

[198] One lawyer attempted to illustrate the difference between permissible real-world activities by an investigator and actions online that would constitute an ethics violation. Clifford F. Shnier, *Friend or Foe?: Social Networking and E-Discovery*, Inside Couns. 2010 WLNR 7382011 (2010) ("If a personal injury defense attorney hires an investigator to take videos of a plaintiff who claims he is incapacitated due to injury, and the investigator catches that plaintiff playing basketball, few courts would disallow that evidence and none would see any reason to discipline the defense attorney. However, if that same defense attorney asks his assistant to 'friend' the plaintiff on Facebook, so as to obtain information that the plaintiff doesn't make available on his page to nonfriends, that crosses the ethical line.").

[199] Martin Cole, *Opinionated*, 66 Bench & B. Minn. 18 (2009).

Without a clear directive from the Model Rules on the issue of social networking in the legal realm, however, many bar associations have simply warned attorneys to tread delicately in this area.[200] As the Dallas Bar Association noted, misrepresenting one's identity in order to become a "friend" on someone's social networking page "could be considered a violation" of the rules of professional conduct.[201] The operative word is *could* because no binding authority has ruled on the issue. It should be noted, nonetheless, that at least one attorney has been admonished by a state ethics board for "friending" an adverse party's Facebook page under false pretenses.[202]

While lawyers are left to guess about the legal ethics of social networking, most articles and opinions on the issue tend to fall in line with the Philadelphia opinion.[203] The common belief is that legal rules governing interaction between lawyers and witnesses in the real world should be the same for online communications. If a certain interaction would be viewed as a lie or as deceptive if it happened face to face, then the same applies to online contacts and "friending" on social networking sites. As one writer summarizes, "Most authorities . . . have found no investigative exception exists to the prohibitions on deception, false statements, or responsibility for the acts of agents or staff when gathering information on adverse parties or witnesses from internet sources."[204]

B. Why Can't We Be Friends?

Another implication of the Philadelphia, Florida, and North Carolina opinions is that the legal world will interpret the word "friend" in a very generic, traditional sense. A friend is a friend, regardless of whether that friendship begins in person or online. The New Jersey Bar Association, for instance, recommends treating a social networking interaction with the same ethical focus as one would an in-person meeting. "A good rule of thumb for attorneys before poking around cyberspace is to consider whether an analogous noncyberspace situation would raise concerns."[205]

Getting a clear understanding of the definition of a "friend" is crucial to determining if online "friendships" violate codes of ethics. The Florida ethics opinion quoted directly from Facebook to help define the parameters and expectations of friendship online.[206] Facebook states that "[y]our friends on Facebook are the same friends,

---

[200] *See, e.g.*, John G. Browning, *What Lawyers Need to Know About Social Networking Sites*, Feb. 1, 2009, http://www.dallasbar.org/about/news-archives.asp?ID=240. ("Beware the ethical pitfalls that lie in attempting to obtain access to such non-public material."); Mara E. Zazzali-Hogan & Jennifer Marino Thibodaux, *Friend or Foe: Ethical Issues for Lawyers to Consider when "Friending" Witnesses Online*, 197 N.J.L.J. 726 (2009) ("Because there is no clear guidance regarding [this], all attorneys should proceed carefully in these circumstances" when investigating witnesses via social networking sites).
[201] *See* Browning, *What Lawyers Need to Know*, Feb. 1, 2009, http://www.dallasbar.org/about/news-archives.asp?ID=240.
[202] Cole, *Opinionated*, 66 Bench & B. Minn. 18 (2009).
[203] *See, e.g.*, Zazzali-Hogan & Thibodaux, *Friend or Foe: Ethical Issues*, 197 N.J.L.J. 726 (2009); John D. Jurcyk, *KBA on Facebook: Blessing or Curse?*, 79 J. Kan. B.A. 8 (2010).
[204] Cole, *Opinionated*, 66 Bench & B. Minn. 18 (2009).
[205] *Quoted in* Zazzali-Hogan & Thibodaux, *Friend or Foe: Ethical Issues*, 197 N.J.L.J. 726 (2009).
[206] Florida Opinion, discussed *supra*, Part II(B).

acquaintances and family members that you communicate with in the real world."[207] But is this truly the reality of how friending on social networking sites works? Having a "friend" on Facebook does not necessarily imply a close personal relationship, after all. One newspaper writer has cleverly argued, "Actual friends and Facebook friends can be as different as leather and pleather."[208] Treating them as synonymous under a generic term of "friendship" unfairly restricts the communication capabilities of judges and lawyers.

Lawyers nationwide are confused about the level of formality and familiarity that a social networking "friendship" implies. One Kansas lawyer wrote about his confusion in defining "friendship" on a social networking site:

> Just what is a Facebook friend? I know what my obligations are to real-life friends. What are the obligations to a digital friendship? I do not even know how to get out of it once I say yes. Of course, once you step over the abyss there is no end in sight. Requests pour in from MySpace, Facebook, Twitter, YouTube, LinkedIn, and many other sites purporting to involve business and/or social settings.[209]

Accepting someone as a friend on a social networking site does not carry with it the same personal connotations as meeting someone in person and talking with them, as noted by the minority in the Florida ethics opinion[210] and by numerous legal commentators.

The legal community has been especially critical of the Florida opinion prohibiting judges from "friending" lawyers that might appear before them.[211] A recent editorial in *Trial Advocate Quarterly* noted the somewhat silly ramifications of the opinion.[212] "[A] judge can have Facebook friends who are not lawyers. A judge can even have friends who are lawyers but who, because of geography, practice specialty, or some other factor, will never appear before that judge."[213] But the opinion draws the line at a lawyer who might appear or had already appeared before that judge.

Lawyers and judges have been put on alert by bar associations and legal publications about the inherent ethical dangers in social networking. Whether they choose to remain "friendly" with each remains to be seen.

---

[207] *Id.* (quoting Facebook materials and warnings).
[208] John Schwartz, *For Judges on Facebook, Friendship Has Its Limits*, N.Y. Times, Dec. 11, 2009, at A25.
[209] John D. Jurcyk, *KBA on Facebook: Blessing or Curse?*, 79 J. Kan. B.A. 8 (2010).
[210] *See* Florida Opinion, *supra*, Part II(B).
[211] *See* John Schwartz, *For Judges on Facebook, Friendship Has Its Limits*, N.Y. Times, Dec. 11, 2009, at A25.
[212] Barbara Busharis, Editorial, *Why Can't We Be Friends?*, 30 No. 1 Trial Advoc. Q. 4 (2010).
[213] *Id.* The author of that article noted that, in light of the opinion, she had been un-friended by one local judge, and she suspected it might occur again as judges attempted to stay on the right side of the ethical line.

IV. Analysis of Social Networking in the Modern Era

In analyzing the three ethics opinions discussed above, I personally find them lacking for two main reasons. First, the reality is that online communications fall short of more personal communications, such as telephone calls or meeting face to face. Making a lawyer treat a "friend" on the Internet the same as she would treat a friend in real life is not reflective of the differences with this type of communication medium. Second, the opinions fail to place any personal responsibility on the page moderator to keep track of her "friends." Unlike letting someone into one's home or office, people are very liberal with whom they will allow to view their pages on Facebook and MySpace. As such, attorneys should be given more ethical leeway to view these sites, as long as they do not use deceptive means to trick the page operator into letting them view the site.

A. Friending Online is Not Friendship in Real Life

Legal experts have labeled the Florida ethics advisory opinion as "hypersensitive" and as an overreaction to the issue of social networking.[214] The results of the opinion seem a bit ridiculous to me. A lawyer cannot be friends with a judge in Florida, but he is free to "friend" a judge in the other 49 states. A judge can be friends with bankruptcy attorneys, as long as he solely tries criminal cases. A judge can play golf with, have dinner with, or even attend a lawyer's wedding – all real life displays of friendship and camaraderie – but that same judge cannot "friend" this same group of lawyers if any of them appear before him in court.

I think the main reason that the Florida opinion is narrowly drawn is because of a lack of understanding of social networking by the older generation.[215] For those that do not regularly use these types of sites, the idea of creating a web page and then only allowing a select group of people to view the full postings seems very personal and private. To the younger generation, though, someone that is accepted as a "friend" online could simply be a random stranger who never becomes more than a name on a "friend" list. Granting access to one's page does not mean granting personal access to one's life, which is the implication of an in-person friendship.

Traditionalists see the word "friend" in the context of social networking and automatically assume that this implicates the codes of ethics that govern communications and relationships between those in the legal community. In the Judge Terry reprimand in North Carolina, the judge there did deserve an admonishment, but it had nothing to do with the fact that he and one of the attorneys in a pending case "friended" each other. Instead, the judge merited a public reprimand because he and the attorney communicated with each other specifically about the case in violation of ethics rules governing ex parte communications. The fact that the judge and attorney had these communications while being "friends" on

---

[214] Schwartz, *For Judges on Facebook, Friendship Has Its Limits*, N.Y. Times, Dec. 11, 2009, at A25.
[215] At least one legal ethics expert also shares this opinion, attributing the difference between the majority and minority views in the Florida ethics advisory opinion to "a generational gap." *See* Schwartz, *For Judges on Facebook, Friendship Has Its Limits*, N.Y. Times, Dec. 11, 2009, at A25. In that article, legal ethics professor Stephen Gillers called the Florida opinion "hypersensitive" to the realities of social networking, and explained that the differences between the majority and minority opinions could be attributed to the varying ages of the committee members.

Facebook, in my opinion, was irrelevant. Had these two men had the exact same conversation in real life, the interaction would have also raised ethical red flags. The medium was not the key issue in that case; the content of the communications between the judge and lawyer was.

Many lawyers and judges have read the North Carolina judicial reprimand, coupled with the ethics advisory opinion in Florida, as a clear mandate to restrict judges from "friending" lawyers completely.[216] Instead, both of these opinions should have focused on the nature of the interaction, and not have issued an outright ban on the place where the interaction took place.[217]

The result may be that lawyers refrain from using social networking sites at all for fear of violating the rules, but I do not view the Model Rules as that narrow. There should be a line between impermissible and permissible conduct online, just as there is in the real world. In the real world, lawyers and judges may golf and attend social occasions together; this doesn't mean there is a perception of favoritism or impropriety. Social networking shouldn't be completely off limits to lawyers just because they are members of a profession that is, in many contexts, often slow to accept technological change.

B. Social Networking is a Public, Not Private, Endeavor

Another misunderstanding regarding social networking is the viewpoint that every access-only social networking site is a private page. The reality, as the Philadelphia lawyer attempted to argue to the ethics advisory committee, is that many MySpace and Facebook users grant easy access to their pages. Although the pages are only viewable to their "friends," this is often not a select group of people (and indeed there seem to be social competitive incentives, as well as hair-trigger "friending" tools built into the technologies, that encourage granting access at high rates). Someone may only invite "friends" to his private home; social networking users allow "friends" of all shapes and sizes to enter their Facebook pages.

The reality of the "industry custom" of social networking usage has obvious implications in the legal world. It is clear that a lawyer, nor a paralegal or investigator working for him, could not go into the adverse party's home or a witness's condo and rummage through desk drawers looking for information for litigation. The same would apply to a witness's car, to her office, or to any space over which she controlled access. There is an expectation of privacy in these areas, and for a lawyer to gain access unlawfully or through deceptive means would be a violation of the Code of Professional Conduct.

The main problem with the advisory opinions discussed above is that they treat a person's Facebook page as if it were the person's home. In the Florida opinion, for example, the Committee quoted Facebook's policies regarding the importance of

---

[216] See Debra Cassens Weiss, *Judge Reprimanded for Friending Lawyer and Googling Litigant*, ABA Journal, June 1, 2009, http://www.abajournal.com/news/article/judge_reprimanded_for_friending_lawyer_and_googling_litigant/.

[217] It could potentially be argued that prohibiting judges from having "friends" in the legal community on their social networking sites is a violation of First Amendment guarantees of both freedom of speech and freedom of association.

maintaining privacy on these pages.[218] Facebook writes, "We understand you may not want everyone in the world to have the information you share on Facebook; that is why we give you control of your information."[219] The site states that it gives users sole control of who they allow to view the most personal parts of their web page, allowing users "to make informed choices about who has access to your information."[220]

I do not believe, however, that this is the reality for most users of social networking sites. Many online "friendships" are granted to total strangers, resulting in a very public display of semi-private information to the world. As such, a traditional view of what "friendship" means in the real world should not be imported into an interpretation of the Model Rules to place unnecessary restraints on lawyers who want to use social networking sites to find information for their cases.

Moreover, I do not view Facebook as a private realm that is heavily guarded by its owner, judging from the pictures and discussions people have on them. Instead, I believe these sites are mediums for exhibitionism at its finest and are used by people to reveal details about their personal lives to people they know, people they kind of know, and people who are complete strangers, all under the common label of "friendship." I believe the younger generation is guilty of oversharing their lives, and I think that social networking sites gives users the perfect medium to reveal very personal details about their lives to a very public audience. It is common knowledge that information from these sites is shared, and it is all-too-easy for someone with access to log-on to the "friend-only" pages and show everyone around the images viewable on his computer screen.

Because of such easy access to someone's personal Facebook page, I do not think it necessarily implies that the Model Rules are violated when a lawyer "friends" a witness that does not know the new "friend" is a lawyer. I interpret "deception" as defined in Rule 4.1 as meaning a lawyer (or those he is responsible for) using *actual* deceptive measures to be granted "friendship" status. The page moderator should be held responsible for whom she allows to view her page, and if she allows complete strangers who just happen to be lawyers to view her page, then the lawyers should not be constrained for collecting the data that they find there. As to those Facebook users who choose to expose their lives to the outside world, they must be held accountable for not doing a very minor inquiry into whom their potential "friends" are. Using deception to gain access to someone's MySpace page should be a violation of the code of ethics; being granted access by asking to be a friend, however, with no lying implied should merely be viewed as good investigative work.

C. A Solution to the Uncertainty of Social Networking?

What is the appropriate solution for dealing with growing ethical issues between the legal community and social networking? Should lawyers and judges lobby the ABA drafters of the Model Rules (or their state counterparts) to include revised wording to address the ethical gray areas exposed by new ways of using technology to communicate, such as social networking?[221] Or do the Model Rules already cast a

---

[218] Florida Opinion, *supra*, Part II(B).
[219] *Id.* (quoting Facebook).
[220] *Id.*
[221] *See* Barbara Busharis, Editorial, *Why Can't We Be Friends?*, 30 No. 1 Trial Advoc. Q. 4 (2010).

wide enough net to encompass interaction online? At least one judge believes that the current rules already give her enough guidance on appropriate ethical conduct without a specific mention of social networking in the rules.[222] The judge says that "her ground rules are simple. She follows her ethical canons and is careful about what she says and who she friends. Yes to all lawyers—to avoid an appearance that she favors one side over another. Friending the general public is trickier. So far, she's been more selective."[223] But what about lawyers and judges that read the Florida ethics opinion or the North Carolina reprimand and decide to stay away from social networking altogether? Is this what the Model Rules require?

The current problem with lawyers using social networking is not disappearing anytime soon. As many bar publications and legal analysts have already begun to note, lawyers should be extremely cautious when using these sites, both when doing research and investigation for litigation, but also when simply keeping up communications with others in the legal profession.[224]

As one bar association recently warned its members, "The rules of professional conduct do not apply any different in the social media context; however, they do still apply. And the informality and ease of use of social media can lull lawyers into acting without thinking, without flexing their judgment muscles."[225] There is, at bottom, a great divide between the traditional view of law and the carefree nature of online activity.[226] For the time being, like other lawyers, I will heed the ambiguous advice of the Dallas Bar Association noted above and "tread carefully" in the social networking realm.

---

[222] *See* Molly McDonough, *Facebooking Judge Catches Lawyer in Lie, Sees Ethical Breaches*, ABA Journal, July 31, 2009, http://www.abajournal.com/news/article/facebooking_judge_catches_lawyers_in_lies_crossing_ethical_lines_abachicago/. At least one lawyer has argued that the rules are "incomplete" regarding the use of social networking in the profession. Steven C. Bennett, *Ethics of Lawyer Social Networking*, 73 Alb. L. Rev. 113, 137 (2009).
[223] McDonough, *Facebooking Judge Catches Lawyer in Lie*, ABA Journal, July 31, 2009 (quoting judge).
[224] Bennett, *Ethics of Lawyer Social Networking*, 73 Alb. L. Rev. at 137 ("With these new networking tools, the practice of law is changing, and rapidly. Social networking requires concerted thinking about adaptation of legal ethics rules to a dynamic world.").
[225] *Quoted in* Helen Hierschbiel, *A Word of Caution: Social Media for Lawyers*, 70 Or. St. B. Bull. 9 (2009).
[226] *See, e.g.*, John Schwartz, *A Legal Battle: Online Attitude vs. Rules of the Bar*, N.Y. Times, Sept. 13, 2009, at A1.

Chapter 3

"Friends," Episode 2: The Wisdom of Discretionary Recusal and the Judge as Actual Friend

Daniel Meyer

Engraved in granite, the quotation above the Criminal Courthouse at the corner of Tulane and Broad[227] reads: "We are a nation of laws, not men." This quote, while accurate in spirit, highlights a fiction in the American justice system. We are, in fact, a nation of laws *and* men.[228] Humans draft, enforce, and adjudicate laws. Laws are subject to human influence at every salient point.

The more pointed question remains: is it possible to truly be "a nation of laws, not men" where laws are discretionarily applied to facts known only by the party, and ruled upon by the very same person adversely affected by the outcome? This question raises the procedure of judicial recusal. Perhaps no other decision in the American justice system is more personal and insulated from the putative cold-blooded nature of law.

Judges, as a function of their human condition and nature, being generally social animals, form interpersonal relationships. For a judge, friendly interpersonal relationships are more of a prerequisite than a correlation. As members of the bar, judges interact and inevitably form friendly interpersonal relationships with other members of the bar community. It is reasonable to conclude that most judges have a friend or two who is a practicing lawyer. When these very same lawyers appear before these same friend-judges, the judge is exposed to a potential ethical issue. Judges have an obligation to preserve the appearance (and reality) of impartially administered justice. Yet a friendship between a judge and a party or lawyer before him can certainly create the appearance of partiality and prejudice.

Neither the federal government, nor the state of Louisiana as but one example on this issue, has passed a statute requiring judges to recuse themselves from cases involving their friends. Lack of notice of the general problem is not to blame for this notable absence. Chief Justice John Marshall declined to recuse himself during the treason

---

[227] Tulane Ave. & S. Broad St., New Orleans, Louisiana 70119. "Tulane and Broad" is the common local nickname for the criminal court of Orleans Parish itself, as in "did you hear about that decision out of Tulane and Broad?"—though to be clear the Tulane half of that moniker has no real connection to Tulane University, miles away. Lawyers are nonetheless grateful that the courthouse is not on Tchoupitoulas Street.

[228] And women, of course. The point is that the courthouse sign raises a false dichotomy and ignores the human reality of law, juries, and judge. In this study, I alternate between *he* and *she* to refer to such persons.

trial of Aaron Burr, and famously played chess with the defendant during his trial.[229] Burr was later acquitted, in 1807. Nearly two centuries later, Justice Antonin Scalia declined to recuse himself from a case even though his friend, Vice President Dick Cheney, with whom the Justice had recently spent two days duck hunting (and survived), was a named party.[230] And on March 11, 2010, the House of Representatives voted unanimously to impeach Judge Thomas Porteous, of the Eastern District of Louisiana.[231] Among the litany of charges against Judge Porteous are accusations that he was coerced into repeatedly ruling in favor of his lawyer-friends, received unreported financial kickbacks from them, and withheld information thereof from the F.B.I.[232]

Lawmakers know that judges occasionally preside over matters in which the party or lawyer is a friend of the judge. Furthermore, history has shown that these same judges can be influenced by the involvement of their friends. There are otherwise-comprehensive recusal statutes, discussed below, which entirely omit the "friend" relationship.

Although many interpersonal relationships trigger automatic recusal, friendship with a party or lawyer will only result in recusal when the judge determines that she is unable to remain impartial as a result of that relationship. When friendship is at issue, a judge in the federal system must recuse himself when either (1) her impartiality might be reasonably questioned, or (2) she has a personal bias or prejudice concerning a party.[233] In Louisiana state courts, by contrast, judges are only *required* to recuse themselves in the first instance—the objective questioning of impartiality. The state's decision to grant a judge this discretion is practical (the judge is best situated to determine his own ability to remain impartial), but it is unclear whether it is wise.

The wisdom of discretionary recusal due to friendship will be analyzed in this paper. In Part I, I introduce the applicable statutory and ethical provisions that apply to judges and lawyers in a friendship relationship. In Part II, I discuss the concept of "friend" and, in Part III, I explore the ethical dilemma friendships may present, in the context of a series of hypotheticals. The shifting and fact-intensive nature of this inquiry, as seen in these hypotheticals, ultimately leads me to the conclusion, in Part IV, that certain aspects of the rule applicable to friendships should remain discretionary.

---

[229] Jeremy M. Miller, *Judicial Recusal and Disqualification: The Need For A Per Se Rule On Friendship (Not Acquaintance)*, 33 Pepp. L. Rev. 575, 578 (2006) (citation omitted).

[230] Miller, 33 Pepp. L. Rev. at 602 (citation omitted).

[231] Nathan Koppel, "House Votes to Impeach New Orleans Judge Porteous," *Wall Street Journal Law Blog* (http://blogs.wsj.com/law/2010/03/11/house-impeaches-new-orleans-judge-porteous/tab/article/), March 11, 2010.

[232] *Id.*

[233] 28 U.S.C. § 455(a); 28 U.S.C. § 455(b)(1) (2009).

I. Statutory Authority and the Judicial Code

A. 28 U.S.C. § 455

Section 455 governs disqualification (recusal) in the federal courts. This section has no procedural component—it is self-enforcing.[234] Parties may file a motion for recusal under § 455, but this practice is surprisingly rare.[235] Judges typically self-assess their relationships with the actors in a case, and determine whether recusal is warranted. Section 455(a) provides that "any justice, judge, or magistrate judge of the United States shall disqualify himself in any proceeding in which his impartiality might be reasonably questioned."[236] Subsection (a) creates an objective standard for disqualification based the *appearance* of partiality, rather than actual partiality. Parties may waive grounds for disqualification under this section.[237]

Section 455(b) enumerates circumstances for disqualification that may not be waived. These circumstances include personal or family financial interest in the matter (beyond a minimal amount), personal knowledge of the disputed facts, and prior involvement in the matter as a lawyer.[238] Subsection (b) also contains two circumstances mandating judicial disqualification which refer to a judge's interpersonal relationships with the actors: (1) where the judge has personal bias concerning a party, and (2) where a judge, his spouse, or a person within the third degree of relationship to either of them, or the spouse of such a person, is a party, lawyer, substantially interested person, or is likely to be a material witness.[239]

This section does not consider disqualification in the event that a friend of the judge is a party or lawyer in the matter. A federal judge's friendship with a party or lawyer in a matter is only grounds for disqualification if, objectively under § 455(a), that judge's impartiality might be reasonably questioned. There is no standalone or mandatory provision dealing with friendships as such.

The applicability of § 455 is pointedly discussed in the Supreme Court's 1993 Statement of Recusal Policy and in Justice Scalia's 2004 memorandum in *Cheney v. United States District Court*.[240] The 1993 Statement of Recusal Policy states that Justices of the Supreme Court will not automatically recuse themselves from cases, "out of an

---

[234] Lori Ann Foersch, *Scalia's Duck Hunt Leads to Ruffled Feathers: How the U.S. Supreme Court and Other Federal Judiciaries Should Change their Recusal Approach*, 43 Hous. L. Rev. 457, 462 (2006) (citation omitted).

[235] Perhaps the reluctance to raise the issue in less-clear contexts derives from the reuted Ralph Waldo Emerson adage (also paraphrased by Omar in HBO's *The Wire*, Season One, 2002, in my final footnote): "If you shoot at a king, you must kill him."

[236] 28 U.S.C. § 455(a) (2009).

[237] *See* 28 U.S.C. § 455(e) ("No justice, judge, or magistrate judge shall accept from the parties to the proceeding a waiver of any ground for disqualification enumerated in subsection (b). Where the ground for disqualification arises only under subsection (a), waiver may be accepted provided it is preceded by a full disclosure on the record of the basis for disqualification.").

[238] 28 U.S.C. § 455(b)(4), (1), (2).

[239] 28 U.S.C. § 455(b)(1), (5).

[240] Cheney v. United States District Court, 542 U.S. 367 (2004).

excess of caution, whenever a relative is a partner in the firm before [the Supreme Court]."[241] Furthermore, the policy statement concludes that Justices "will not recuse [themselves] by reason of a relative's participation as a lawyer in earlier stages of the case.... [They] shall recuse [themselves] whenever... a relative has been lead counsel below."[242] The 1993 Statement of Recusal Policy thus narrowly interprets § 455(b)(5)(ii),[243] which states that a judge *must* recuse himself if "a person within a third degree of relationship" to the judge or his spouse is "*acting* as a lawyer in the proceeding."[244]

Justice Scalia's memorandum in response to the Sierra Club's motion to recuse him from *Cheney v. United States District Court* further demonstrates the Supreme Court's tendency to narrowly apply § 455(a). In January 2004, three weeks after the Supreme Court granted *certiorari* in the *Cheney* case, Justice Scalia participated in a two-day duck hunting trip in rural Louisiana with Vice President Cheney.[245] Thirteen people attended the hunt, including Justice Scalia, his son, and son-in-law.[246] Justice Scalia and his family members flew to Louisiana on *Air Force 2* with the Vice President, and returned via commercial flight.[247] The Sierra Club, and much of the national media, argued that the relationship between Justice Scalia and Vice President Cheney, a named party in a matter before the Supreme Court, fundamentally triggered § 455(a).

Section 455 does not require a judge to document his reasoning on the record. Justice Scalia's memorandum, therefore, was written on his own volition. Justice Scalia provided both a legal justification and a policy reason for his decision not to recuse himself. As a legal reason, Justice Scalia employed the "Microsoft Recusal Interpretation," which relates the perspective of § 455(a) to that of a reasonable observer who is informed of *all* the surrounding facts and circumstances.[248] Justice Scalia concluded, based on his recounting of all the circumstances of his duck hunting trip with the Vice President, that his impartiality could not be reasonably questioned, and therefore that recusal under § 455(a) was not required.[249]

As a matter of policy, Justice Scalia pointed out that recusal is tantamount to a vote for the Respondent.[250] Because the Petitioner needs five votes to overturn a lower court's decision, recusal automatically reduces the available votes to eight. The Supreme Court's 1993 Statement of Recusal Policy and Justice Scalia's memorandum

---

[241] *Cited in* Foersch, 43 Hous. L. Rev. at 467 (citation omitted).

[242] *Id.* (quoting policy) (bracketed material by Daniel Meyer, for clarification).

[243] *See* 28 U.S.C. § 455(b)(5)(ii). It is apparent to me that this is one example of a narrowing construction of the statute, which, for example, does not in terms distinguish lead counsel.

[244] 28 U.S.C. § 455(b)(5)(ii), *as quoted in* 43 Hous. L. Rev. at 469-70 (emphasis added by Daniel Meyer).

[245] Foersch, 43 Hous. L. Rev. at 470 (discussing background facts of case cited above).

[246] *Id.* at 471.

[247] *Id.*

[248] *Id.* at 473-74.

[249] *Id.* at 474-75 (citation omitted). *See* Cheney v. United States District Court, 542 U.S. 367 (2004).

[250] Cheney v. United States District Court, 542 U.S. 367, 367 (2004); Foersch, 43 Hous. L. Rev. at 476 (citation omitted).

both suggest a policy of resolving gray area disputes against recusal. Ultimately, when the case was decided, Justice Scalia sided with the Vice President.

B. Canon 2 of the Code of Judicial Conduct: The Louisiana Regulations

Louisiana state court judges and judicial officers must comply with the Code of Judicial Conduct, a set of ethical rules for judges first promulgated by the American Bar Association and adopted in some form among the various states. Canon 2 of the Code of Judicial Conduct instructs judges to avoid both impropriety, and the appearance of impropriety, in all activities.[251] Section A requires Louisiana judges to "act at all times in a manner that promotes public confidence in the integrity and impartiality of the judiciary."[252] Section B specifically prohibits a judge from allowing "family, social, political, or other relationships to influence judicial conduct or judgment."[253]

Although no judge is entirely insulated from her surroundings, it is reasonable to prohibit a judge from allowing interpersonal relationships to "influence" her judicial conduct or judgment. Canon 2 does not mandate recusal or disqualification. It does, however, regulate a judge's conduct and judgment. If that conduct or judgment is influenced by a social relationship, the judge is in violation of this section.

C. Canon 3C

Canon 3C governs recusal of Louisiana judges. This section states that a judge should "disqualify himself or herself in a proceeding in which the judge's impartiality might be reasonably questioned and shall disqualify himself or herself in a proceeding in which disqualification is required by law or applicable Supreme Court rule."[254] This section applies the same objective standard of the federal statute, 28 U.S.C. § 455(a), here as to Louisiana state judges.

D. Rule 8.4

In addition to regulating friendships from the judicial side of that equation, states through their bar organizations and courts, and in adopting model ethics rules suggested by the ABA, may also regulate the lawyer as friend. For example, attorneys in Louisiana must adhere to the Rules of Professional Conduct.[255] Rule 8.4 enumerates specific instances that amount to professional misconduct. Subsection (e), in particular, provides that it is misconduct to "state or imply an ability to influence improperly a judge... to achieve results by means that violate the Rules of Professional Conduct or other law."[256] It is also professional misconduct to "knowingly assist a judge ... in conduct that is a violation of applicable Rules of Professional Conduct or other law."[257]

---

[251] Code of Judicial Conduct, Louisiana, Canon 2.
[252] Canon 2, Section A.
[253] Canon 2, Section B.
[254] Canon 3C, Code of Judicial Conduct, Louisiana (as amended through August 1, 2008).
[255] Rules of Professional Conduct, Louisiana (as amended through October 1, 2009).
[256] Rules of Professional Conduct 8.4(e).
[257] Rules of Professional Conduct 8.4(f).

II. Friendship as a Legally Cognizable Relationship

In order to focus the conversation about the merits of recusal based on friendship, it is necessary to provide a concrete definition of "friendship." This task is difficult because, unlike familial or business relationships, friendship is a fluid and dynamic relationship. A spouse will remain a spouse, unless there is an abrupt change (divorce or death). A law partner will remain a law partner unless the partnership is dissolved. Friendship, however, is subject to the ebb and flow of the relationship. Friendship is not a formal relationship, nor is it memorialized in writing. Individuals are generally able to personally assess who is a friend and who is not. However, individual standards will inevitably vary. In order to apply a term legally, the definition must be articulated. To introduce this articulation, I turn to the scholars.

Friendship is a "relational term which signifies something about the quality and character of the relationship involved."[258] In Plato's *Lysis*, the philosopher describes the quality and character of the relationship as a kind of love where people generally assist one another.[259] Professor Charles Fried defines a friend as one who acts in the interest of another over his own.[260] In *Nichomachean Ethics*, Aristotle states that friends are people who wish their counterparts well for their friend's own sake.[261] A dictionary defines a friend as "one well known to another and regarded with affection and loyalty; an intimate supporter."[262]

More particularly as to this context, Professor Jeremy Miller, in his *Pepperdine Law Review* article, defines friendship, for recusal purposes, as loyalty to one side of a case (be it a named party or lawyer), triggered by an intimacy beyond social or business collegiality (mere politeness).[263] This definition comports with the common thread in the above-cited definitions of friendship, as well as a common sense interpretation of the word: friendship implies loyalty. Loyalty implies partiality. Miller suggests a *per se* recusal rule: "friendship between a judge and a named party or attorney of record, that exceeds ordinary and reasonable social intercourse between acquaintances and business associates, mandates judicial recusal."[264]

III. Application of Recusal Law to Hypothetical Situations

A. Big City, Big Firm

Hypothetical facts, drawn from my locale but likely translatable to many similar jurisdictions: two lawyers from different law schools start working the same week at the New Orleans branch of a national law firm. Over 75 attorneys work in the firm's

---

[258] Ethan J. Lieb, *Friendship and the Law*, 54 UCLA L. Rev. 631, 638 (2007) (citation omitted).

[259] As discussed in Jeremy M. Miller, *supra, Judicial Recusal and Disqualification*, 33 Pepp. L. Rev. at 587 (citation omitted).

[260] *Id.* at 588 (citing Fried's classic work on the adversarial role of lawyers and the analogy of *friend* that he uses to explore role morality).

[261] Lieb, 54 UCLA L. Rev. at 650 (citation omitted).

[262] Miller, 33 Pepp. L. Rev. at 587 (citation omitted).

[263] *Id.* at 579.

[264] *Id.* at 578-79.

New Orleans office. These lawyers rise through the ranks of the law firm, and make partner within 18 months of each other. The first lawyer, Jerry, is magnetic inside the courtroom and out, making friends with everyone from the Entergy Centre doorman, to his secretary, to the Governor of Louisiana. The second lawyer, Bob, is affable but primarily family-oriented. He is acquainted with politicians, but not on a first-name basis. Jerry and Bob are regular golf partners, and their families vacation together biannually.

Eventually, Jerry is appointed to a federal judicial vacancy in the Eastern District of Louisiana. Bob leaves the law firm to start his own practice one year after Jerry's appointment, bringing with him a large shipping company involved in a major Jones Act case. The company's boat sank in the Mississippi river, and all seventeen seamen aboard perished. The plaintiffs will settle for $85 million. The shipping company disputes liability, and the matter goes to trial. Jerry is the presiding judge. Jerry and Bob have not spoken since the case was removed to federal court. At no point during his tenure at the law firm did Jerry do any work for the shipping company, and he has no personal financial stake in the matter.

As a federal judge, Jerry's recusal decision is governed by 28 U.S.C. § 455. Under § 455(a), recusal may be based on the objective questioning of impartiality.[265] Under § 455(b), the only relevant ground for recusal is subsection (1), where a judge "has a personal bias or prejudice concerning a party."[266] If recusal is warranted under § 455(b)(1), then certainly also the so-called Microsoft interpretation of § 455(a)—a reasonable observer aware of *all* the circumstances—would mandate recusal. Subsection (a) casts a wider net than (b); it is a catch-all provision. Thus the recusal decision boils down to whether an objective observer could question Jerry's impartiality. It takes a great deal of honesty to admit that, in light of all the circumstances, one's own impartiality is objectively questionable. It takes a great deal of hubris to suggest that one's own integrity is so unflappable that it would dissuade the suspicious, objective observer.

Justice Scalia's own hubris may have impacted his reasoning in declining to recuse himself from *Cheney v. United States District Court*. Many reputable media outlets and the Sierra Club questioned Justice Scalia's impartiality based on his relationship with Vice President Cheney. There *were* parties questioning Justice Scalia's impartiality. By refusing to recuse himself, Justice Scalia was suggesting that either the parties questioning his impartiality were not objective, or that they were not aware of all the circumstances.

i. Personal Application of Law and Experience to the Facts

If I were the judge, Jerry, in this matter, I would not recuse myself under § 455(b)(1). Admitting my own personal bias is a difficult and uncomfortable exercise, and even then I may believe in good faith that I could judge impartially. I would, however, recuse myself under § 455(a). An objective observer would no doubt question my impartiality, given the extensive nature of my friendship with the lawyer. Even if I do not consider Bob the Lawyer a friend, the objective standard will still trigger recusal.

---

[265] 28 U.S.C. § 455(a), discussed in Part I(A) above.
[266] 28 U.S.C. § 455(b)(1).

In this hypothetical, recusal is permissible but not required, depending on degrees of the facts. By accounting for "all the circumstances," the objective observer's perspective necessarily incorporates the character of the judge involved.[267] Importantly, the character of the judge is both a relevant circumstance for the objective observer (under the Microsoft interpretation), and creates context to interpret facts (Judge Porteous' impartiality can be objectively questioned under less extreme facts than those involving other judges). If I believe, as the judge in this hypothetical, that a reasonable observer familiar with all the circumstances would question my impartiality, I must recuse myself. Conversely, if I do not believe as much, I might not recuse myself. It requires an uncommon level of self-awareness and lack of ego for a judge to determine, without any meaningful supervision, that his impartiality might be objectively questioned.

My instinct compels me to deny recusal. Impartiality is an outcrop of self-control. I believe, and *want* to believe, that I could manage to maintain an impartial courtroom for the duration of a trial involving even my closest friend. But I am not sure. If the case took a sharply negative turn against my friend Bob the lawyer, and it appeared that his only client (a fact known to me from our history) stood to lose the full $85 million, I cannot be entirely certain that I would not act, consciously or subconsciously, in his assistance. My actions may not be as blatant as ruling in his favor, but I may be unwittingly tempted to strong-arm a settlement or delay the case, effectively to treat the case differently from my normal routine though in ways in which others may not perceive to be either bias nor a negative result for the non-friend client. (Or it is even possible I would bend over backwards against Bob, and hold him to deadlines and page limits I do not enforce on many others, just so that no one could question my partiality.) In this vein, it is fair to ask why Justice Scalia would even *care* that his recusal would tip the balance toward affirmance, if he is judicially indifferent to the case and its outcome.

Recusal laws are drafted from the objective perspective to avoid these types of problems. Humans, and judges, don't necessarily control their subconscious mind. The human brain, imbued with levels of consciousness, functions at its highest state when instinct, the id, is overpower by objective consciousness—the super-ego. Therefore, I must defer to my objective determination of impartiality and recuse myself.

Professor Miller's proposed rule that "friendship between a judge and . . . attorney of record, that exceeds ordinary and reasonable social intercourse between acquaintances and business associates, mandates judicial recusal" helpfully removes the discretionary element from the hypothetical.[268] Under § 455(a), presently, the judge must make a broad determination of objective impartiality, without the aid of any significant guideposts concerning friendship. Under Miller's rule, the judge must only decide whether his relationship with the advocate "exceeds ordinary and reasonable social intercourse between acquaintances." In short, the judge must make

---

[267] It may be argued that the telescoping focus of the perspective of the objective observer in the Microsoft recusal interpretation (awareness of all the facts and circumstances) ultimately limits the available field of persons *qualified* to apply the objective standard to one: the judge herself.

[268] *See* Miller, 33 Pepp. L. Rev. at 578-79.

what could be called a *playground decision* and decide whether the advocate is his friend or not. Applying Miller's rule, there is no gray area in my decision to recuse from the above hypothetical.

ii. Altering the Hypothetical Facts

When a matter of degree of facts determines the outcome, context is critical. If Jerry and Bob's families do not vacation together, and they do not play golf regularly, it becomes more difficult to objectively question Jerry's impartiality. If Jerry and Bob are work friends, but do not regularly fraternize outside of the office, Jerry should not recuse himself. If Jerry has impartially presided over Bob's cases in the past with no hint of prejudice, then the argument for objective impartiality is weaker.

If Jerry were a state court judge in the original hypothetical, he should not recuse himself from the equivalent state case involving Bob the Lawyer. Under state law, Jerry is prohibited under Canon 2 from allowing Bob's involvement to influence his judicial conduct or judgment. Additionally, under Rule 8.4, Bob may not state or imply an ability to influence the judge because they are old friends. If Jerry is a state judge in New Orleans, Canon 3C would govern recusal. Canon 3C uses a similar objective impartiality inquiry to § 455(a), and similar reasoning will apply. However, the question of whether facts concerning a friendship objectively demonstrate the appearance of impartiality is fundamentally altered in the state court context, in many jurisdictions much like Louisiana. The civil district court judge in Orleans Parish is an elected office. By virtue of the electoral process, elected judges will (and often must) have many close friends in the bar community.

In New Orleans, the Court's familiarity with a practitioner appearing before it is not uncommon. The civil district court docket is jam-packed, and practitioners may repeatedly appear before the same judge. As a practical matter, judges need certain latitude when hearing cases involving their friends as parties or lawyers. A bright-line rule regarding friendship might force very popular judges to recuse themselves from an untenable percentage of cases. As a policy matter, it makes sense to allow state judges, in whom enormous public trust is already vested, to determine when to recuse themselves. In private life, friends will tend to demonstrate loyalty. However, in the public eye of the adversarial system, and with the dragnet of the court of appeal looming, loyalty will tend to give way to professionalism and impartiality in the courtroom. For these reasons, I would not recuse myself from this hypothetical case if it were in state court.

Three key differences lead to the varying hypothetical outcomes in state and federal court. First, federal judges are appointed by the President and confirmed by the Senate, not elected. Second, federal jurisdiction covers a narrower spectrum of the law than state courts, but also covers a larger geographic and population base. Third, federal court dockets are typically less crowded than their state counterparts. These three differences create a different context through which facts must be viewed when making a recusal decision. Context being critical, the outcome is also different.

Another contextual note that could also make a difference in responsible analysis and judicial administration: New Orleans and the federal Eastern District of Louisiana are jurisdictions with large populations that permit judicial recusal without significant deprivation of court services. There are many lawyers and judges in New

Orleans. In smaller jurisdictions, recusal can effectively deny a claimant his access to court.

B. Bon Temps, Louisiana

Facts: In the hypothetical town of Bon Temps, Louisiana, there are seven lawyers, and one judge. The single judge, Jerry, presides over all matters, civil and criminal. For federal matters, Bon Temps residents must travel to Monroe, Louisiana. Jerry regularly presides over cases involving all seven of Bon Temps' lawyers. One of the seven attorneys, Bob, is a childhood friend of Judge Jerry. Jerry and Bob have known each other their entire lives. Their wives are in a book club together, and their sons play on the same baseball team. Bob, a personal injury lawyer, has tried 20 cases in front of Jerry. Bob has won impressive verdicts in all 20 cases, and has a tendency to win borderline evidentiary matters. Now Bob is trying an unwitnessed "slip and fall" action on behalf of an injured plaintiff. After discussing Bob's impressive and suspicious track record before Judge Jerry, the defense (out-of-town lawyers) moves for recusal.

As a state judge in Louisiana, Jerry's decision to recuse himself is governed by Canon 3C. Canon 3C provides two grounds for disqualification: (1) the objective appearance of impartiality, or (2) where disqualification required by law or Supreme Court rule.[269] The objective appearance of impartiality is reached through analysis of all relevant circumstances. Bob and Jerry's friendship might be grounds for recusal in a big city, but in a small town like Bon Temps, everyone knows everyone. The same friendship (and track record) that would certainly require recusal in New Orleans falls into an ethical and legal gray area in Bon Temps. If I were the judge in this hypothetical, based only on the information given, I would deny the motion to recuse. Although there is a strong argument that my impartiality may be objectively questioned, I will deny the motion to recuse. I must not deny the litigant his forum and attorney of choice. Absent violation of the mandatory rule for bias and the like, it is my obligation to simply do my best to impartially preside over the case, to not allow the jury to be prejudiced, and to check my instinctive loyalty to my old friend Bob.

IV. Conclusion

A dishonest judge will find a way to manipulate his position for personal gain. A bright-line rule requiring recusal based on friendship will prevent an honest judge from behaving unethically. Prejudice or bias towards a party or lawyer by a judge is already barred in federal courts and the state of Louisiana. The only gain made by a *per se* recusal rule based on friendship is an immeasurable one: the degree to which a judge's judicial conduct or judgment is not affected in his subconscious mind by his familiarity with a party or lawyer in a matter. This gain is ultimately illusory.

Recusal based on friendship is analogous to case screening in a prosecutor's office. It is more effective and efficient to dismiss bad cases before they have a chance to be tried, and clog the justice system. Similarly, it is more effective to screen out partial judges at the outset of a case rather than to set up guidelines within the case limiting

---

[269] Canon 3C, Code of Judicial Conduct, discussed above in Part I(C).

the judge's potential for prejudicial influence. However, when the judge is the key party determining the appropriateness of recusal, the determination of his lack of impartiality is subject to his own ethical candor. Logically, this process does not make sense. Practically, it makes perfect sense. Only the judge really knows all the circumstances (and so, he is the only surrogate for the objective observer).[270] In the absence of an omniscient arbiter of facts, I conclude that recusal based on friendship is an appropriately discretionary process.

---

[270] "If you shoot at the king, you best not miss." – Omar Little, *The Wire*, noted above.

Chapter 4

"Friends," Episode 3: Appearance of Impropriety, Judges on Facebook, and the Modern Day Contact Rolodex

Renee Goudeau

The *appearance of impropriety* standard in the Code of Judicial Conduct has a long history met with proponents and opponents vigorously arguing about the standard. It has seen one of its most interesting applications, recently, on the question whether a judge may ethically have "friends" on Facebook and other social networking sites in the same manner, and to the same extent, as those who are not controlled by the judicial code and do not wear the robes. Part I traces the history of the appearance of impropriety standard to its present form. Part II summarizes the various viewpoints of proponents and critics of this standard. In Part III, I discuss this standard as it relates to online social networking, and consider recent and competing decisions in Florida and South Carolina on the subject. Finally, in Part IV, I analyze the social networking situation under the appearance standard, and I conclude that states like Florida which have begun to crack down on the judge's having Facebook friends actually misperceive the virtual relationships involved, quite possibly from a generational gap.

I. History

In its first efforts at regulating judicial conduct, the American Bar Association ("ABA") did not impose any rule that threatened judges with disqualification, removal, or even discipline because of the "appearance of impropriety."[271] The ABA moved from fatherly advice, to aspirations, to stronger cautions—and eventually, after much debate, to the present proposal that the ABA is now advocating for implementation among the states.[272]

In 1924, the ABA House of Delegates promulgated the first judicial code, called the Canons of Judicial Ethics.[273] The actual title of Canon 4 of the 1924 Canons was "Avoidance of Impropriety." This Canon provided, among other rules and guidelines, that "a judge's official conduct should be free from impropriety and the appearance of

---

[271] Ronald D. Rotunda, *Judicial Ethics, the Appearance of Impropriety, and the Proposed New ABA Judicial Code*, 34 Hofstra L. Rev. 1337, 1352 (2006).

[272] *Id.* That version is discussed and analyzed further below.

[273] *Id.*; American Bar Ass'n, About the Commission, Background Paper, *ABA Joint Commission to Evaluate the Model Code of Judicial Conduct*, http://www.abanet.org/judicialethics/about/backround.html (last visited March 13, 2010). To see the product of this Commission, see Canons of Judicial Ethics (1924), *reprinted in* Lisa L. Milord, The Development of the ABA Judicial Code 131-43, at 132 (1993).

impropriety,"[274] and it also advised that the judge, in his everyday life out of court, should be "beyond reproach."[275]

Almost fifty years later, the ABA House of Delegates replaced these Canons with the 1972 Code of Judicial Conduct.[276] Many states soon adopted the model 1972 Code, subject of course to various non-uniform amendments. The 1972 Judicial Code used the term "should" instead of the more statutory and mandatory "shall."[277] Thus, the title to Canon 2 read: "A Judge Should Avoid Impropriety and the Appearance of Impropriety in All His Activities.[278] The Reporters' Notes advised that "the black-letter statement of Canon 2 is very broad in its terms and perhaps the nearest to being horatory of any provision in the code."[279]

This long-term move to mandatory rule rather than mere aspirational guideline continued next with the 1990 version of the ABA Code of Judicial Conduct.[280] The drafting committee in the 1990's replaced the "should" with the emphatic "shall" and expanded its reach to include the judge's action and roles even when she is off the bench, not acting in her capacity as judge.[281] Thus, the title of Canon 2 of the 1990 Code provided: "A Judge Shall Avoid Impropriety and the Appearance of Impropriety in All of the Judge's Activities."[282] But this requirement was still the *title* to Canon 2 rather than one of the rules under Canon 2.[283] The legislative history advised that the purpose of this expanded rule was "to caution judges to avoid certain prospective conduct even if the conduct only appears suspect, and to proscribe any act that is harmful even if it is not specifically prohibited in the Code."[284] References to "cautioning" the judge in the ABA Model of Judicial Conduct signaled that this part of the Canons was merely aspirational.

In 2007, the ABA again revised its Model Code of Judicial Conduct.[285] "During the revision process, the Commission solicited comments on a number of provisions that

---

[274] ABA, About the Commission, Background Paper, *ABA Joint Commission to Evaluate the Model Code of Judicial Conduct*.
[275] *Id.*
[276] Rotunda, *Judicial Ethics, the Appearance of Impropriety, and the Proposed New ABA Judicial Code*, 34 Hofstra L. Rev. 1337, 1352 (2006). The Preface to the 1972 Judicial Code said: "The canons and texts establish mandatory standards unless otherwise indicated." Code of Judicial Conduct Preface (1972), *quoted in* Center. for Prof'l Responsibility & Judicial Div., ABA, Annotated Model Code of Judicial Conduct, 4 (2004), E. Wayne Thode, Reporters' Notes to Code of Judicial Conduct 5 (1973).
[277] Rotunda, 34 Hofstra L. Rev. at 1352.
[278] Thode, Reporters' Notes to Code of Judicial Conduct 8 (1973).
[279] *Id.* at 49.
[280] Rotunda, 34 Hofstra L. Rev. at 1353.
[281] *Id.*; Model Code of Judicial Conduct Canon 2 (1990); Milord, *supra*, The Development of the ABA Judicial Code 13 (1993).
[282] Rotunda, 34 Hofstra L. Rev. at 1353.
[283] *Id.*
[284] *Id.*
[285] Nancy J. Moore, *Is the Appearance of Impropriety An Appropriate Standard For Disciplining Judges in the Twenty-First Century?*, 41 Loy. U. Chi. L.J. 285, 285 (2010); and Model Code of Judicial Conduct (2007). This is an excellent article to understand the pros and cons of an appearance

had provoked extensive discussion and controversy in Commission hearings and meetings," including the appearance of impropriety standard.[286] The Commission wavered, waffled, or (more charitably) mediated between those who urged retaining the appearance of impropriety standard and those who argued in favor of eliminating it. In February 2007, the Commission issued its report to the ABA House of Delegates retaining the admonition that judges should avoid the appearance of impropriety, "but only in the language of Canon 1 itself, not in one of the several black-letter rules under Canon 1."[287] On February 7, 2007, the Conference of Chief Justices of the state supreme courts added its own emphatic voice on the issue of appearance of impropriety: the Conference sharply opposed the Commission's Final Report "due to its failure to provide for the enforcement of the prohibition on creating the appearance of impropriety."[288] The Conference of Chief Justices implied in terms that no one misunderstood that if the Commission did not amend its proposed code in line with the justices' position on the issue, then they would withhold political support for the new code—"thereby making it unlikely that it would be adopted in more than a few states. Not surprisingly, the Commission backed down and revised its report," wrote one expert observer of the process, Professor Nancy Moore.[289]

The ABA Joint Commission has now expanded the "appearance of impropriety" standard not only as the title to Canon 1, but further as a specific, separate rule under that Canon, Rule 1.02. In the present form, Canon 1 reads: "A Judge Shall Uphold and Promote the Independence, Integrity, and the Impartiality of the Judiciary, and Shall Avoid Impropriety and the Appearance of Impropriety."[290] In addition, Rule 1.2, entitled "Promoting Confidence in the Judiciary," states that "a judge shall act all times in a manner that promotes public confidence in the independence, integrity, and impartiality of the judiciary, and shall avoid impropriety and the appearance of impropriety.[291] The Commentary to the Canon defines the phrase by an objective test, stating that "an appearance of impropriety occurs when reasonable minds with knowledge of all the relevant circumstances disclosed by a reasonably inquiry,

---

standard, and (as with Professor Rotunda's, *supra*, in arguing against the standard) also the procedural background to the current rule.

[286] *Id. See also* Memorandum from Mark I. Harrison, Chair, ABA Joint Commission to Evaluate the Model Code of Judical Conduct to Individuals and Entities Interested in Judicial Ethics 1-3 (May 11, 2004), *available at* http://www.abanet.org/judicialethics/memo_canon1_051104.pdf, *cited in* Moore, 41 Loy. U. Chi. L.J. at 285 n.3.

[287] Moore, *supra*, 41 Loy. U. Chi. L.J. at 286, *citing* ABA Joint Comm'n to Evaluate the Model Code of Judicial Conduct, Report to the ABA House of Delegates 4 (Dec. 20, 2006), *available at* http://www.abanet.org/judicialethics/house_report.html.

[288] Moore, 41 Loy. U. Chi. L.J. at 285-86, *citing* Conference of Chief Justices, Resolution 3; Opposing the Report of the ABA Joint Commission to Evaluate the Model Code of Judicial Conduct in Light of Its Failure to Provide for Enforceability of the Canon on "appearance of impropriety" (Feb. 7, 2007), *available at* http://ccj.ncsc.dni.us/JudicialConduct Resolutions/resol2AppearanceOfImpropriety.html.

[289] Moore, 41 Loy. U. Chi. L.J. at 287. Professor Moore would certainly understand the process and politics of such a promulgation exercise, as she herself had once served as the chief ABA Reporter on a committee that was tasked with fundamentally redrafting rules of lawyer conduct.

[290] Model Code of Judicial Conduct Canon 1 (2008).

[291] *Id.* R. 1.2.

conclude that the judge's honesty integrity, impartiality, temperament, or fitness to serve as a judge is impaired."[292] As Professor Moore later tallied: "All of the state courts in which the 2007 Judicial Code has either been adopted or recommended appear to have retained the appearance of impropriety as an enforceable standard, in accordance with the view of the Conference of Chief Justices."[293] Today, any lawyer—and even the media or blogs—can accuse a judge of violating the "appearance of impropriety" in either his private or official capacity because the Title of Canon 1 and the Rule 1.2 itself decidedly tell us that the judge must avoid such appearances.

In stark contrast to this restriction on, and standard for, judges, the ABA explicitly considered and rejected a similar "appearance of impropriety" standard as applied to *lawyers* in 1983, when the Model Rules of Professional Conduct were promulgated.[294] Indeed, this rejection was one of the more obvious changes from the previous Model Code of Professional Responsibility, which had used such language, as had much case law. Any disqualification for an appearance of impropriety for lawyers historically was used to decide the specific allegation that a lawyer was involved in a conflict of interest, not really as some general rule of ethics for other contexts. It has been argued that lawyers have no similar clearly articulated duty, unlike judges.[295] Lawyers owe varying and contextually-specific duties to clients (and prospective clients); to courts and judges; to third persons who may be affected by the lawyer's or client's actions, and even to the public at large.[296] Even harder to pin down, these duties owed to different actors in the legal system may themselves conflict, often requiring resort to a specific Model Rule just to decide which "duty" controls in such cases.[297] So it must be recognized that the lawyers' ethics standards, unlike the judicial code, simply do not have any *general* rule prohibiting lawyers from committing an "impropriety" or "appearance of impropriety."

II. Competing Viewpoints on the Judicial Appearance of Impropriety Standard

Proponents of the appearance of impropriety standard for the judiciary maintain that judges, as "neutral decision-makers," thus "have a single, clearly articulated duty to conduct themselves with independence, integrity, and impartiality."[298] Under the 2007 Judicial Code, then, an actual impropriety "means judicial conduct that in fact compromises the independence, integrity, and impartiality of a judge."[299] In turn,

---

[292] *Id.*
[293] Moore, 41 Loy. U. Chi. L.J. at 287-88, *citing* Center for Prof'l Responsibility Pol'y Implementation Comm., Comparison of ABA Model Judicial Code and State Variations 1 (Aug. 25, 2009), *available at* http://abanet.org/cpr/code/1_2.pdf.
[294] Rotunda, *supra*, 34 Hofstra L. Rev at 1344-51.
[295] Moore, 41 Loy. U. Chi. L.J. at 290, 292, *citing* Model Rules of Prof'l Conduct pmbl. 1 (2008).
[296] Moore, 41 Loy. U. Chi. L.J. at 292.
[297] *Id.*
[298] Moore, 41 Loy. U. Chi. L.J. at 290, *citing* ABA Joint Comm'n to Evaluate the Model Code of Judicial Conduct, Reporters' Explanation of Changes 7 (2007), *available at* http://www.abanet.org/judicialethics/mcjc-2007.pdf.
[299] Moore, 41 Loy. U. Chi. L.J. at 290-91, *citing* Model Code of Judicial Conduct Terminology 5-7 (2008).

appearance of impropriety means judicial conduct that appears, to a reasonable person, to compromise the judiciary's independence, integrity, and impartiality as well.[300] "Avoiding not only impropriety, but also the appearance of impropriety, is important for judges because public confidence in the independence, integrity, and impartiality of the judiciary is critical to the public's willingness to accept judicial decision-making and submit to the rule of law."[301]

Professor Moore uses a perfect case law example from close to home: a Louisiana state court judge once showed up to a Halloween party, held in a public restaurant, in black-face, donned in an orange prison jumpsuit and wearing handcuffs; guests, patrons, and staff (including African American workers) all saw the judge's conduct.[302] No evidence of actual bias in his judicial role was shown, but the public display "clearly created the appearance that he was prejudiced against blacks and would not be impartial when they appeared before him as parties."[303] This example clearly goes to the proponents' view that this appearance of impropriety would lead African Americans, and more generally all observers, to have less confidence in the integrity of the judicial system.

The critics of the appearance of impropriety standard argue that it is a vague and subjective standard that imposes excessive and unnecessary burdens. The standard hinges discipline on " 'the whim of judicial disciplinary authorities,' "[304] it " 'chill[s] courageous and innovative judicial decision-making,' "[305] and it "makes it difficult for judges to predict how the standard will apply."[306] Some courts have certainly expressed their own concerns about the possible vagueness of the appearance of impropriety standard:

> Propriety, however, is often in the eye of the beholder. A given individual will find conduct to be within or beyond the bounds of propriety to the extent the conduct comports with the individual's own highly subjective views of propriety.... Disciplinary rules expressed in terms of "propriety" risk mercurial existence rising and falling with the temper of the moment. Such rules place *ipse dixit* powers, antithetical to rule of law, in the hands of disciplinary boards and courts applying such rules.[307]

---

[300] Moore, *supra*, at 291, *citing* Model Code of Judicial Conduct R. 1.2 cmt. 3 (2007).
[301] Moore, *supra*, at 291.
[302] *Id.* She analyzes *In re* Ellender, 889 So.2d 225, 227 (La. 2004). But to quote Elle Woods in *Legally Blonde* (2001): "Whoever said orange was the new pink was seriously disturbed."
[303] Moore, 41 Loy. U. Chi. L.J. at 292. *See In re* Ellender, 889 So.2d at 229 (agreeing).
[304] Moore, 41 Loy. U. Chi. L.J. at 295. She is quoting from page 6 of an APRL Letter from Ronald C. Minkoff and Ronald E. Mallen, Assoc. of Prof'l Responsibility Lawyers ("APRL"), to ABA Commissions on the Model Code of Judicial Conduct (June 30, 2004), at 6, *available at* http://www.abanet.org/judicialethics/resources/comm_rules_minkoff_063004.pdf.
[305] Moore, 41 Loy. U. Chi. L.J. at 295, *quoting* APRL Letter at 7. The brackets are Professor Moore's; she is summarizing some of the criticisms of the standard rather than her own view, of course.
[306] Moore, *supra* , at 295. This view is particularly argued by Professor Rotunda, *supra*, 34 Hofstra L. Rev. at 1342-44; *see also* Leslie Abramson, *Appearance of Impropriety: Deciding When A Judge's Impartiality "Might Reasonably Be Questioned*," 14 Geo. J. Legal Ethics 55 (2000).
[307] *In re* Larsen, 616 A.2d 529, 580-81 (Pa. 1992) (per curiam).

Critics thus say that the unnecessarily imprecise ethics rules allow legal actors and the public, with minimum effort and no specific rule violations, to bring a legitimate charge that the judge has violated the ethics rules.[308]

As Professor Ronald Rotunda, one of the more clear and consistent voices in opposition to the appearance standard, has argued: "Overuse not only invites abuse with frivolous charges that have the patina of legitimacy, but also may eventually demean the seriousness of a charge of being unethical."[309] The standard thus not only tells judges to behave (if not *how* to), it further empowers participants in the process to bring motions for recusal based not on a showing of a clear rule violation, but rather the violation of the mandatory prohibition against appearing to have impropriety.

The debate will continue not only among scholars and in court decisions, but also within various state organizations in deciding whether to adopt the latest version of the Judicial Code for that jurisdiction and its judiciary.

III. Online Social Networking and the Appearance of Impropriety

Today, online social networking sites, such as MySpace, LinkedIn, and Facebook, have given a new sense of discomfort to judicial ethics committees. Various ethical problems may certainly arise with membership from these sites, and some are beginning to be addressed. Ethics commissions have taken on the task of establishing boundaries for judges who become members of these sites.

One of the primary reasons people use social networking sites is to share their content with others. For example, the Facebook mission statement is "to give people the power to share and make the world more open and connected."[310] Social networking sites, such as Facebook and MySpace, have various means people can share and control information. First, the site can be used to identify a member's "friends." Second, the site can be used by members to keep updated on birthdays, post pictures, and web videos of their "friends"—and also to comment on a friend's page or "wall." Third, the sites allow members to view other material that their friends have elected to appear on their own personal site such as their updated status, groups, interest, and activities; the member's telephone number or email address; her school or workplace; and even that member's "relationship status." Fourth, and finally, social networking sites have privacy settings allowing the member to limit the information he shares with friends and others. The member must also accept a person who requests to be identified as that member's "friend."

Recently, the Florida Judicial Ethics Advisory Committee has stated that judges cannot add lawyers, who may appear before them, as "friends" on Facebook or similar sites, while not completely foreclosing judges and attorneys from belonging to the same online groups.[311] This opinion was specifically limited to judges.[312] At the heart

---

[308] *See* Rotunda, 34 Hofstra L. Rev. at 1338.
[309] *Id.*
[310] http://www.facebook.com/policy.php (last visited May 20, 2010).
[311] The Florida Defense Lawyers Association, Judicial Ethics Advisory Committee: No "Friending" Judges, 30 No. 1 Trial Advoc. Q. 22, 22-23 (2010).

of the opinion regarding judges is a concern that being listed as a judge's friend provides an image to the public that particular lawyers are in a position of special influence, while also giving the appearance of impropriety.[313]

The Committee held that a judge who identifies lawyers that may appear in front of the judge as a "friend," on the judge's page and permits those lawyers to identify the judge as a "friend" on their pages, violates Canon 2B.[314] The Committee reasoned that a judge's ability to accept or reject a lawyer as a "friend"—and the online communication between the judge and the lawyer "friend" to others—is at its essence what violates Canon 2B, because it conveys or gives the impression that the judge's lawyer-"friends" are in a special position to influence that judge.[315]

As previously stated, any site member has the ability make a friendship request, accept or reject friendship requests, and communicate through various means with her "friends." This begs the question, for all practical purposes: does a judge's mere acceptance or rejection of a lawyer as a "friend" gives the impression of a special influence to a judge? Also noteworthy, as seen below, is that the Florida judicial opinion stresses the acceptance or rejection of a lawyer as friend as creating an appearance of impropriety. However, the opinion does not state what types of communication would or would not be permissible if a judge and lawyer communicated via a message board in a group that they both belonged to on the online social networking site.

The Committee went further than Canon 2B in justifying its decision by relying on various sources and canons. The Committee admitted that "judges cannot isolate themselves from the real world and cannot be expected to avoid all friendships outside their judicial responsibilities," yet "some restrictions upon a judge's conduct are inherent in the office." However, in analyzing the commentary on Canon 2A, it concluded that having lawyers who may appear before a judge as his "friend" would create the appearance of impropriety.[316]

---

[312] In a later opinion, issued very recently, the Florida Judicial Ethics Advisory Committee stated that judicial assistants may "friend" lawyers on social networking sites. The opinion stated that "as long as a judicial assistant utilizes the social networking site outside of the judicial assistant's administrative responsibilities and independent of the judge, thereby making no reference to the judge or the judge's office, this Committee believes that there is no prohibition for a judicial assistant to add lawyers who may appear before the judge as 'friends' on a social networking site." The Florida Defense Lawyers Association, Judicial Ethics Advisory Committee: Whether the inquiring judge should require the judicial assistant to refrain from adding lawyers who may appear before the judge as "friends" on a social networking site, 2010-04 (March 19, 2010).
[313] The Florida Defense Lawyers Association, Judicial Ethics Advisory Committee: No "Friending" Judges, 30 No. 1 Trial Advoc. Q. 22, 22 (2010).
[314] Id. at 22-23. (Canon 2B of the judicial ethics code states: "A judge shall not lend the prestige of judicial office to advance the private interest of the judge or others; nor shall a judge convey or permit others to convey the impression that they are in a special position to influence the judge.")
[315] Id. at 23.
[316] Id. (Canon 2A states: "Irresponsible or improper conduct by judges erodes public confidence in the judiciary. A judge must avoid all impropriety and appearance of impropriety. A judge must expect to be the subject of constant public scrutiny. A judge must therefore accept

Additionally, the opinion notes that the social networking sites are broadly available for the general public view and access on the internet. Therefore, "it is clear that many persons viewing the site will not be judges and will not be familiar with the code or recusal provision or other requirements which seek to assure the judge's impartiality."[317] The Committee also recognized that the judge's participation in a social networking site must also conform to the general limitations imposed by Canon 5A, which provides:

> A judge shall conduct all of the judge's extra-judicial activities so that they do not
>> a. Cause reasonable doubt on the judge's capacity to act impartially as a judge
>>
>> b. Undermine the judge's independence, integrity or impartiality
>>
>> c. Demean the judicial office
>>
>> d. Interfere with the proper performance of judicial duties
>>
>> e. Lead to frequent disqualification of the judge; or appear to a reasonable person to be coercive.[318]

Using this analysis, on the other hand, the Committee could have alternatively concluded that since so many of the members of the general public use social networking, the public realizes that the term "friend" on social networking sites has a looser interpretation than does the judicial ethics committee interpretation.

Finally, the Committee stated that "the issue is not whether the lawyer *actually* is in a position to influence the judge, but instead whether the proposed conduct, the identification of the lawyer as a 'friend' on the social networking site, *conveys the impression* that the lawyer is in a position to influence the judge."[319] Additionally, the Committee limited its opinion as it related to lawyers who *may* appear before the judge.[320] Therefore, the holding does not apply to the "friends" of judges who are not lawyers, or lawyers who do not appear before the judge because they do not practice in the judge's courtroom or the judge has listed them on the recusal list.[321]

In sum, there are many problems and unresolved questions related to the opinion. For example, the first is whether or not lawyers who are "friends" with judges actually creates an appearance of impropriety. Second is the lack of acknowledgement in the types or a standard to apply to the communications between a lawyer and judge on a social networking site that may create an appearance of impropriety. Finally, the fact that the opinion had to use three different general canons to conclude that lawyers who are "friends" with judges gives

---

restrictions on the judge's conduct that might be viewed as burdensome by the ordinary citizen and should do freely and willingly.")
[317] The Florida Defense Lawyers Association, Judicial Ethics Advisory Committee: No "Friending" Judges, 30 No. 1 Trial Advoc. Q. 22, 23 (2010).
[318] *Id.*
[319] *Id.* at 24 (emphasis added).
[320] *Id.*
[321] *Id.*

the appearance of impropriety actually shows, in my opinion, the inherent weakness of the opinion.

In a vigorous dissent, the minority view of the Committee concluded that "listing of lawyers who may appear before the judge as 'friends' on a judge's social networking page does not reasonably convey to others the impression that these lawyers are in a special position to influence the judge and does not violate Canon 2B."[322] The minority reasoned that social networking sites have become so ever-present in the general population's daily routine and activities that the term "friend" on these sites simply does not have the same meaning as it once did in the pre-internet age.[323] In the minority members' view, the term "friend" can be identified as a "contact or acquaintance," and does not convey that the person is a "friend" in the traditional sense.[324]

The majority opinion also addresses other issues such as judge-to-judge contact on a social networking site, whether or not election campaign materials may be posted on behalf of a judge's candidacy on a social networking site, and whether or not lawyers, who may or may not appear before a judge, can become a "fan" of a judge's candidacy or their election campaign materials on a social networking cite. The Committee answered these questions in the affirmative, allowing lawyers and judges to continue to participate in these types of activities because it does not reasonably convey the impression of an appearance of impropriety.[325] The irony of allowing a lawyer, who may or may not appear before a judge, to become a "fan" of the judicial candidacy—but forbidding a lawyer and judge to become "friends"—is not lost upon anyone.

In stark contrast to the Florida opinion, the South Carolina Advisory Committee on the Standards of Judicial Conduct concluded that a judge may be a member of Facebook—and can also be friends with law enforcement officers and employees of the magistrate as long as they do not discuss anything related to the judge's position as magistrate.[326] The reasoning follows that permitting a magistrate judge to be a member of a social networking site allows the community to see how the judge communicates and gives the community a better understanding of the judge.[327]

IV. Analysis

As seen from the above, the appearance of impropriety standard has been criticized by judges and lawyers alike. Lawyers and judges are often confused about the boundaries and limits on what is the actual standard for the "appearance of impropriety." The standard has been criticized for its vagueness and limitless potential for over-reaching. For example, judges disciplined for engaging in the "appearance of impropriety" are more often than not also punished for some other

---

[322] *Id.*
[323] *Id.*
[324] *Id.*
[325] *Id.*
[326] The South Carolina Judicial Department, Advisory Committee on Standards of Judicial Conduct, Op. 17-2009 (Oct. 2009).
[327] *Id.*

ethical violation, such as appearance of partiality.[328] This leaves some to question whether this standard is actually needed because it is accompanied by another violation.

However, proponents make the point that the standard keeps the public faith in the confidence in our judicial system. In arguing to the keep the standard, they state that specific rules cannot cover all situations which may come before an ethics council and also that it is difficult to prove that a judge has actually engaged in actual impropriety. Therefore, the standard is in place for unique circumstances which often create the appearance of impropriety, and this standard helps to keep public confidence in our judges.

Furthermore, the recent opinion by the Florida Judicial Ethics Committee has discussed the appearance standard in regards to a new modern digital age. The Committee concluded that judges who are "friends" with lawyers (who may appear before them) on online social networking sites, such as Facebook, give the appearance of impropriety.[329] I would actually agree with the minority opinion that judges and lawyers merely being "friends" does not create an appearance of impropriety.[330] I think my difference of opinion may stem from age or a generational gap. Generational differences have always existed throughout history. However, with the emergence of the internet and a new digital age, there has been a rapid change in culture with respect to internet usage, communication, and politics.

The primary difference between the generations is the internet. The younger generation has grown up using the internet and computers as a primary source of communication and information. Therefore, they are more comfortable using the internet and "chatting and friending" online. In contrast, the older generation did not grow up using the internet, but had to learn to use computers in their workplace. Therefore, they are generally not as versed in internet lingo, communication, and culture.

Another major difference between the generations is the definition of the word "friend." Older generations may associate friends with the traditional sense: a close friend, family member, or neighbor. However, Facebook and other social networking sites have a much larger population of younger members than older members. Many young people on Facebook have upwards of 1,000 friends. The term "friend" on Facebook is used very loosely, most of these friends would be considered by older generations as acquaintances.

Facebook "friends" are now what I consider to be the *"modern day contact rolodex."* The term "friend" on Facebook and other social networking sites is not always associated with close friends, but sometimes merely "acquaintances." In my opinion, as a young Facebook member, I would not consider a judge who is merely "friends" with a

---

[328] *See, e.g.*, Huffman v. Arkansas Judicial Discipline & Disability Comm'n, 42 S.W. 3d 386 (Ark. 2001). The Arkansas Supreme Court held that a judge's ownership of a retailer's stock created an appearance of impropriety and recusal was required, even if ownership interest was *de minimus*.
[329] The Florida Defense Lawyers Association, Judicial Ethics Advisory Committee: No "Friending" Judges, 30 No. 1 Trial Advoc. Q. 22, 22 (2010).
[330] *See id.* at 23.

lawyer to create an appearance of impropriety. However, the leaders in the legal community are generally from the older generation, and this may be one of reasons why the Florida opinion was decided the way it was.

With that being said, a lawyer who frequently writes on a judge's "wall," posts pictures of social gatherings with the judge, and belongs to the same groups as the judge, would create the appearance of impropriety. But, how much would be too much? There could be no way to measure how many times a lawyer writes on the judge's wall or posts pictures, and thus whether or not this would create the appearance of impropriety. This result may itself arise because the standard could be considered vague and subjective. However, there could be virtually no way of monitoring or setting a standard regulating such "Facebooking" activities. Therefore, it is probably in the judiciary's best interest to set a firm prohibition against lawyers, who may appear before a judge, to be "friends" with a judge on an online social networking website.

V. Conclusion

There has been a heated debate for years regarding the appearance of impropriety standard. With all the arguments, differing opinions, commentary, and disagreements regarding the standard, it is apparent that the proponents have won the battle for the standard. Its application to new situations and technologies, however, is not so settled. In conclusion, one thing is certain: the appearance of impropriety standard is here to stay.

Chapter 5

The Problem of Circumventing the Labor Management Reporting and Disclosure Act by Using the Ancillary Business Model

J. Ryan Lopatka

In recent years, lawyers looking to expand the scope of their profession and diversify their practices have turned to establishing ancillary businesses to offer nonlegal services such as tax preparation, title services, and human resource consulting. One of the primary benefits of such arrangements is that the attorney or law firm can offer a one-stop shop for clients needs. Due to the burgeoning interest of firms to enter into such arrangements, in 1992 the American Bar Association adopted Rule 5.7 of the Model Rules of Professional Conduct, in order to address potential ethical issues resulting from the operation of such ancillary businesses. State bar associations that have adopted and implemented Rule 5.7 have generally interpreted the rule as allowing attorneys to establish ancillary businesses to offer law-related services, but the states differ as to how other ethical rules may apply to the lawyer and business. Moreover, most jurisdictions have scarce case law regarding ethical rules that arise when a firm chooses to establish an ancillary business.

One particular scenario that courts and state bar associations may need to address in the near future concerns labor law firms creating labor consulting firms. This area may prove to be an interesting application of Rule 5.7, perhaps with unintended side effects. With the Obama administration slated to pass legislation aimed at expanding the scope of the Labor Management Reporting and Disclosure Act, labor law firms could foreseeably create an ancillary business arrangement to provide their clients with labor advice while circumventing the disclosure requirements contemplated by the new legislation. Depending on the character and structure of such businesses, ethical requirements engendered by the Model Rules present important issues regarding the treatment of confidential information, client referrals, and advertising and solicitation.

I. Background

Section 203(b) of the Labor Management Reporting and Disclosure Act ("the Act" or "LMRDA") requires a law firm or consulting firm to file an annual report with the Secretary of Labor identifying all the firm's clients, as well as the receipts and disbursements from the respective clients for all labor relations work, if the firm engages in "persuader" activities.[331] "Persuader" activities as defined by the LMRDA connote any activities in which the object is "to persuade employees to exercise or

---

[331] 29 U.S.C. § 433, Section 203(b) (2010).

not to exercise, or persuade employees as to the manner of exercising, the right to organize and bargain collectively through representatives of their own choosing."[332]

Although there is a split among the federal circuit courts, the Department of Labor ("DOL") has adopted the position that the disclosure requirement pertains to all firm clients receiving labor relations advice or services, and not merely the clients with which they engage in persuader activities. [333] However, to balance this onerous disclosure requirement, Section 203(c) of the Act includes an exception to the rule for such firms that give or agree to give advice to an employer.

The interpretation of the *advice exception* has been openly disputed over the past twenty years with regard to its treatment of union campaign materials. Since 1962, the advice exception has covered not only an attorney's reviewing and revising campaign materials drafted by the employer, but also the preparation of campaign materials so long as the employer has the opportunity to reject the attorney's handiwork.[334] In the closing days of the Clinton administration, the DOL revised this 40-year-old interpretation to remove the preparation of campaign materials from the advice exception altogether, thereby subjecting any law firm that drafts campaign materials for an employer to the requirements within Section 203(b).[335] The narrowed Clinton DOL exception never took hold, however, as President Bush's incoming administration stayed the interpretation on February 9, 2001, soon after entering office,[336] and eventually rescinded the interpretation entirely, on April 11 of that year.[337]

More recently, President Obama's administration issued a Notice of Proposed Rule Making on December 7, 2009, which took the position that the current advice exception within Section 203(c) is overbroad and slated a revision of the rule to take place in November of 2010.[338] The new rule will most likely revive the Clinton Labor Department's interpretation, but could possibly make the exception even narrower.

Consequently, in order to draft campaign materials and sidestep the disclosure requirements of Section 203(b) that they may perceive as burdensome or intrusive, labor law firms may contemplate offering these services through a wholly or partly owned ancillary business. Following a model similar to the one used by Barnes & Thornburg, an Indianapolis based law firm that partnered with FlashPoint HR

---

[332] 29 U.S.C. § 433, Section 203(b)(5)(1) (2010).
[333] Various circuit courts starting in 1965 split on this interpretation. Donovan v. The Rose Law Firm, 768 F.2d 964, 975 (8th Cir. 1985); Humphreys, Hutcheson & Moseley v. Donovan, 755 F.2d 1211, 1222 (6th Cir. 1985); Master Printers Ass'n v. Donovan, 699 F.2d 370, 375 (7th Cir. 1983); Price v. Wirtz, 312 F.2d 647, 651 (5th Cir. 1969); Douglas v. Wirtz, 353 F.2d 30, 34 (4th Cir. 1965). *See also* 29 U.S.C. § 433, Section 203(c) (2010), ameliorating the effect.
[334] Charles Baird, *It Depends on What the Meaning of "Advice" Is*, COLUMNS, (May 1, 2001), *available at* http://www.thefreemanonline.org (last visited, Mar. 27, 2010).
[335] Interpretation of the "Advice" Exemption in Section 203(c) of the Labor-Managment Reporting and Disclosure Act, 66 Fed. Reg. 8, 2782 (Jan. 11, 2001).
[336] Interpretation of the "Advice" Exemption in Section 203(c) of the Labor-Managment Reporting and Disclosure Act, 66 Fed. Reg. 28, 9724 (Feb. 9, 2001).
[337] Interpretation of the "Advice" Exemption in Section 203(c) of the Labor-Managment Reporting and Disclosure Act, 66 Fed. Reg. 70, 18864 (Apr. 11, 2001).
[338] Interpretation of the "Advice" Exemption in Section 203(c) of the Labor-Managment Reporting and Disclosure Act, 74 Fed. Reg. 233, 64268 (Dec. 7, 2009).

Consulting in 2002 to offer human resources services to its clients, a labor law firm may similarly partner with a consulting firm consisting of nonlawyers in order to draft campaign materials for its clients.[339] Alternatively, the law firm could start its own ancillary business or wholly purchase such a business for these purposes. If a labor law firm were to pursue one of these options in order to offer clients services that constitute "persuader" activities, the resulting business arrangement would raise various ethical issues, particularly as to Model Rule 5.7 concerning the responsibilities of law firms and associations regarding law-related services.[340]

II. Rule 5.7 on Ancillary Businesses and Related Rules of Conduct

Promulgated in 1992 by the American Bar Association, Rule 5.7 of the Model Rules of Professional Conduct ("Model Rules") addresses the circumstances under which a law firm may offer law-related services to clients. In pertinent part, Rule 5.7 reads:

> (a) A lawyer shall be subject to the Rules of Professional Conduct with respect to the provision of law-related services, as defined in paragraph (b), if the law-related services are provided:
>
> > (1) by the lawyer in circumstances that are not distinct from the lawyer's provision of legal services to clients; or
> >
> > (2) in other circumstances by an entity controlled by the lawyer individually or with others if the lawyer fails to take reasonable measures to assure that a person obtaining the law-related services knows that the services are not legal services and that the protections of the client-lawyer relationship do not exist.[341]

Effectively, Model Rule 5.7 assumes that a law firm may create a separate entity to offer law-related services and creates a rebuttable presumption that whenever a lawyer provides law-related services or controls an entity that provides such services, the ethical rules will apply.[342]

If a labor law firm creates a subsidiary company or enters into a partnership with a consulting company to engage in persuader activities, and more particularly, to draft campaign materials, the first inquiry would be whether the persuader activities are

---

[339] This example is illustrated by *Services: Human Resource Consulting* (Barnes & Thornburg, LLP ed. 2010), *available at* http://www.btlaw.com/ServiceArea.asp?Section=Services&ServiceArea_ID=37.
[340] ABA, Model Rules Prof'l Conduct R. 5.7 (2010), *available at* http://www.abanet.org/cpr/jclr/rule.charts.html (hereinafter "MRPC").
[341] *Id.*
[342] Katharyn A. Thompson, *The Real Deal-Breakers: Lawyers Must Operate Ancillary Businesses Within the Boundaries of Ethics Rules*, 90 A.B.A. J. 26, 26 (2004); *see, e.g., Charts Comparing Professional Conduct Model Rules as Adopted or Proposed by States to ABA Model Rules* (ABA, Mar. 2010), *available at* http://www.abanet.org/cpr/jclr/rule_charts.html (last visited, Apr. 14, 2010) (Thirty-three states have adopted atleast some variation of Model Rule 5.7. The remaining seventeen states generally agree that all ethical rules apply to the law-related services provided by ancillary businesses, which has the same basic effect as if Model Rule 5.7 were adopted.).

law-related services. Comment 9 to Model Rule 5.7 lists a broad range of services considered to be law-related, such as "providing title insurance, financial planning, accounting, trust services, real estate counseling, legislative lobbying, economic analysis, social work, psychological counseling, tax preparation, and patent, medical or environmental consulting."[343] The gamut of services the American Bar Association thus denotes as law-related does not explicitly include labor consultation, but the list is not exhaustive.

Model Rule 5.7(b) itself defines law-related services as "services that might reasonably be performed in conjunction with and in substance are related to the provision of legal services, and that are not prohibited as unauthorized practice of law when provided by a nonlawyer."[344] For services to fall under the definition, they must satisfy two basic requirements: one, the services must be performed in conjunction with and related to the provision of legal services, and two, when provided by a nonlawyer, the services must not amount to the unauthorized practice of law.[345] Persuader activities likely satisfy both prongs of the definition.

First, performing services such as drafting and reviewing campaign materials relates to and is in conjunction with the provision of legal services a labor law firm may render. For example, employers seeking legal advice regarding their employees in a union setting often ask attorneys to review campaign materials. In an analogous context, the Boston Bar Association found human resources consulting related to and in conjunction with a law firm's legal services because the firm had previously rendered these services as part of its legal representation.[346]

Second, many persuader activities including drafting and revising campaign materials do not constitute the unauthorized practice of law when rendered by nonlawyers. The Ohio Supreme Court addressed the issue holding that in the event a nonlawyer offers advice in collective bargaining matters, including the drafting of non-legally binding instruments, such practices are are not classified as unauthorized practices of law.[347] Additionally, the U.S. Court of Appeals for the Fourth Circuit, in *Douglas v. Wirtz*, noted as early as 1965 that persuader activities do not necessarily amount to the practice of law.[348] Piggy-backing off this rationale in a modern setting, labor consulting firms that consist of nonlawyers currently do exist to offer such services and are generally not viewed as players in the legal profession.

Because persuader activities—particularly drafting and revising campaign materials—satisfy the two requirements of Model Rule 5.7, these services when offered by a labor law firm's ancillary business are likely to be considered law-related. As a result, Rule 5.7 suggests that if a lawyer or law firm's ancillary business offers law-related services, other rules of professional conduct will apply as well. A labor law firm forming a separate entity to offer persuader services therefore must

---

[343] MRPC 5.7, cmt. 9 (2010).
[344] MRPC 5.7(b).
[345] *Id.*
[346] Boston Bar Association, *Ethics Opinion 199-B: Law-Related Services (LRS)*, 43 Boston Bar J. 16, 16 (1999).
[347] Ohio State Bar Ass'n v. Burdzinski, 858 N.W.2d 372, 377 (Ohio 2006).
[348] *See Douglas v. Wirtz*, 353 F.2d 30, 33 (4th Cir. 1965).

consider important issues regarding confidentiality (Model Rule 1.6), client referrals (Rule 1.8), advertising (Rules 7.1 and 7.2), and solicitation (Rule 7.3).

A. Model Rule 1.6: Confidentiality

If a labor law firm forms an ancillary business to engage in persuader activities, a serious and recurring question arises as to the treatment of information passed between the employees of the ancillary business and its customers. Rule 1.6, relating to a lawyer's duty of confidentiality, reads: "a lawyer shall not reveal information relating to the representation of a client unless the client gives informed consent, the disclosure is impliedly authorized in order to carry out the representation" or in other situations where the lawyer feels the disclosure is reasonably necessary.[349] But Model Rule 1.6, including all its accompanying comments, does not provide any guidance as to whether a nonlawyer employee of an ancillary business owned by lawyers owes the same duty of confidentiality to her client as a lawyer would. On the other hand, comment 10 to Rule 5.7 suggests that when a lawyer provides law-related services, he must "scrupulously adhere" to the confidentiality rules.[350] Although most jurisdictions which have implemented or applied Rule 5.7 adhere to the strict approach embodied in comment 10, the rule and comment simply does not address a general ethical standard relating to ancillary businesses and the release of information, and so at least one jurisdiction has read and analyzed this issue differently.[351]

One rather unique approach to the confidentiality issue turns on the employment status of the ancillary business nonlawyers offering the services. In an ethics opinion regarding the professional conduct rules applying to an ancillary human resources consulting firm, the Boston Bar Association opined that if the nonlawyers providing the services to the customer were not also employees of the parent law firm, Rule 1.6 would not apply to their communications.[352] This would mean that, absent informed consent, the law firm could not share the confidential information of its clients with the ancillary entity, because they would not be considered employees of the law firm for the purposes of Rule 1.6.[353] On the other hand, if the nonlawyers were employees of the law firm, Rule 1.6 would apply to their communications with the ancillary business's customers just as the rule would apply to paralegals, secretaries, and other nonlawyer staff of a law firm.[354] A labor law firm opening an ancillary business for persuader services in Boston would therefore want to make the consultants of the ancillary business employees of the law firm if the firm wished to create a free exchange of information between the law firm and the consulting firm.

---

[349] Model Rules Prof'l Conduct R. 1.6(a) (2009), *available at* http://www.abanet.org/cpr/jclr/rule.charts.html.
[350] MRPC 5.7, cmt. 10.
[351] *See Would you like a financial plan with that?*, Eye on Ethics (ABA, ed. 2006), *available at* http://www.abanet.org/media/youraba/200602/article01.html (last visited, May 21, 2010). *See generally* Boston Bar Association, *Ethics Opinion 199-B: Law-Related Services (LRS)*, 43 Boston Bar J. 16, 16 (1999).
[352] Boston Bar Ass'n, 43 Boston Bar J. at 28.
[353] *Id.*
[354] *Id.*

B. Model Rule 1.8: Referrals and Disclosing Business Interests

Client referrals raise ethical issues regarding business transactions with clients. A labor law firm looking to avoid the disclosure requirements of Section 203(b) by forming an ancillary business to handle persuader activities will likely want to refer clients to its persuader business and vice versa. Comment 5 to Model Rule 5.7 reads: "When a client-lawyer relationship exists with a person who is referred by a lawyer to a separate law-related service entity controlled by the lawyer, individually or with others, the lawyer must comply with Rule 1.8(a)."[355] As the ABA in Rule 5.7 suggests, a client referral from a law firm to its ancillary counterpart triggers Rule 1.8, which implicates situations that give rise to a conflict of interest. Subsection (a) of Rule 1.8 states:

> A lawyer shall not enter into a business transaction with a client or knowingly acquire an ownership, possessory, security or other pecuniary interest adverse to a client unless: (1) the transaction and terms on which the lawyer acquires the interest are fair and reasonable to the client and are fully disclosed and transmitted in writing in a manner that can be reasonably understood by the client; (2) the client is advised in writing of the desirability of seeking and is given a reasonable opportunity to seek the advice of independent legal counsel on the transaction; and (3) the client gives informed consent, in a writing signed by the client, to the essential terms of the transaction and the lawyer's role in the transaction, including whether the lawyer is representing the client in the transaction.[356]

Seemingly, under the Model Rules of Professional Conduct, an ancillary business may refer a customer to its parent law firm without prompting any ethical obligation on the part of the lawyers in the firm. However, when the firm refers a client to its ancillary business, it must cure the inherent conflict of the transaction by disclosing the terms of the transaction, advising the client to seek independent counsel, and obtaining informed consent in writing from the client. Most jurisdictions follow this model.[357]

A jurisdiction approaching the ancillary business model for the first time may choose to view the ethical obligations arising from client referrals more liberally. The Boston Bar Association takes the view that a lawyer must comply with Rule 1.8 only if the lawyer has an ownership interest in the ancillary business to which he refers the client.[358] Therefore, under this interpretation, an attorney in the law firm with no direct interest in the ancillary business could ethically refer a client without adhering to the disclosure requirements within Rule 1.8(a). This distinction effectively eviscerates Rule 1.8 in many typical situations, because the firm could easily have its

---

[355] MRPC 5.7, cmt. 5.
[356] Model Rules Prof'l Conduct R. 1.8(a) (2010), *available at* http://abanet.org/cpr/jclr/rule.charts.html. Some jurisdictions, through case law or as an interpretation of fiduciary duty, have even more specific and onerous requirements in such situations.
[357] John S. Dzienkowski & Robert J. Peroni, *Conflicts of Interst in Lawyer Referral Arrangments with Non-Lawyer Professionals*, 21 Geo. J. Legal Ethics 197, 211 n.79 (2008).
[358] Boston Bar Association, *Ethics Opinion 199-B: Law-Related Services (LRS)*, 43 Boston Bar J. 16, 28 (1999); *see also* Stephanie Francis Ward, *Top 10 Ethics Traps*, 93 A.B.A. J. 30, 30 (2007).

first-year associates make all client referrals and sidestep the conflict issue altogether.

Despite the Boston Bar Association's unique treatment of client referrals in the ancillary business context, a labor law firm referring its clients to its ancillary persuader firm would want to take steps to purify the transaction of any perceived impropriety (or for that matter, an actual one, especially if the jurisdiction is one that would apply Rule 1.8 broadly to this context or otherwise has case law compelling higher disclosure). Thus, the attorney making the referral should, at the very least: (1) inform the client that the firm had an ownership interest in the consulting firm (or perhaps disclose what indirect interest he or she holds); (2) advise the client to seek independent counsel with regard to the transaction; and (3) obtain written, informed consent of the client that he understands that the law firm has an interest arising out of the referral to the ancillary business.

There would seem to be no compelling reason to avoid making full disclosure and obtaining the proper client consent, even if it could be ethically avoided by some interpretations or with second-hand referrals. And indeed complying with Rule 1.8 and similar law seems to be good business practice as well, if only to highlight the range of services the law firm and its associated entity can offer and make clear the separate roles of each part.

C. Model Rules 7.1 and 7.2: Advertising

A labor law firm will likely want to advertise in some manner the persuader services offered by its ancillary consulting firm, in order to market its distinctive services and the advantage of its having different specialized entities. Comment 10 to Model Rule 5.7 notes in the promotion of its ancillary business, a firm must comply with Rule 7.1, which addresses communications of the lawyer's services, and Model Rule 7.2, addressing a lawyer's ethical responsibilities in the realm of advertising.[359] Therefore, pursuant to Rule 7.1, communications regarding the ancillary business's services must not be false or misleading, and pursuant to Rule 7.2, the firm cannot exchange anything of value for the recommendation of its services and all advertising communications must contain the name and address of at least one firm member responsible for its content.[360] The strict rules adopted by the ABA (and the tendency of state bars to enforce rules in this area strictly) make clear that lawyers must tread especially carefully in the self-promotion of their legal services. And comment 10 to Rule 5.7 suggests that the same care be taken by the firm's ancillary business.

Pennsylvania, a state that has adopted a rule similar to ABA Model Rule 5.7, subscribes to the rule embodied in comment 10. For example, an attorney forming an ancillary business offering mediation services sought guidance from the Pennsylvania Bar Association concerning the ethical obligations arising from the proposed

---

[359] MRPC 5.7, cmt. 10.
[360] Model Rules Prof'l Conduct R. 7.1, 7.2 (2010). Because implementation of advertising rules varies greatly among the states, and is subject to constitutional review in the courts, those firms wishing to advertise their one-stop-shopping package will need to carefully consider the relevant jurisdictions' rules, procedures, and case law on advertising (and solicitation, below), beyond the general strictures of the suggested Model Rules in this area.

business arrangement. The Pennsylvania Bar determined that the attorney must also comply with Rules 7.1 and 7.2 when advertising his services as a mediator.[361]

On the other hand, the Boston Bar Association, noted above for its liberal treatment of client referrals to ancillary businesses, found Rule 7.2 regarding advertising to be generally *inapplicable* to ancillary businesses so long as the business is separate and distinct from the legal practice of the parent firm.[362] If, however, the separate business entity advertised its affiliation with the law firm, the advertisement must not run afoul of Rule 7.1 by misleading customers of the ancillary business.[363] Likewise, if the advertisement serves as marketing for both the law firm and the ancillary business, the advertisement must comply with all ethical rules that ordinarily apply to advertising undertaken by law firms.[364]

In every jurisdiction, then, the envisioned labor law firm that establishes an ancillary persuader consulting firm must at least be mindful of a potential ethical violation when advertising its separate business entity. In order to abide by the ABA's rules of conduct and the various jurisdictions' likely implementation of them, the firm should advertise its ancillary business by the same standards that it advertises the law firm.

Under no circumstances can the advertisement make a misrepresentation of law or fact nor can it omit a fact that would render the advertisement misleading to a potential client. Notwithstanding the Boston Bar Association's interpretation that Rule 7.2 does not apply to the advertisements purely of the ancillary business, a labor law firm should be careful not to give anything of value to another person for recommending the firm or ancillary business's services and should, among other features, include in any advertisement the name and office address of at least one attorney responsible for the advertisement.

D. Model Rule 7.3: Solicitation

Ethical issues related to advertising and marketing also may arise if the labor law firm *solicits* clients for the law firm or ancillary business. Model Rule 7.3 prohibits attorneys from soliciting professional employment (in all but a few enumerated circumstances) when the attorney's primary motive is pecuniary in nature.[365] Again, comment 10 to Model Rule 5.7 provides a glimpse into the ABA's intent and suggests that an ancillary business shall abide by the same standards as a law firm concerning the ethical bounds of solicitation of new clients.[366] Moreover, in such circumstances where the attorney may solicit employment, the attorney must indicate the mailings or electronic communication as "Advertising Material."[367]

---

[361] Ethics Digest, *Mediation: Responsibility Regarding Nonlegal Services*, 19 Penn. Lawyer 41, 41 (1997).
[362] Boston Bar Association, *Ethics Opinion 199-B: Law-Related Services (LRS)*, 43 Boston Bar J. 16, 28 (1999).
[363] *Id.*
[364] *Id.*
[365] Model Rules Prof'l Conduct R. 7.3(a) (2010), *available at* http://www.abanet.org/cpr/jclr/rule.charts.html.
[366] *See* MRPC 5.7, cmt. 10.
[367] MRPC 7.3(c). As with advertising and Rule 7.2, state bar and state court implementations of the rules on solicitation (and even the definition of the activity) vary widely and must be checked before acting. The issue here is whether those restrictions and the case law

Recall the above-referenced scenario in which the attorney requested an opinion concerning the ethical repercussions of establishing an ancillary business as a mediator. The Pennsylvania Bar Association further advised that Rule 7.3 restricting an attorney's ability to solicit business applies in equal force to an ancillary business.[368] Similarly, in a final advisory opinion dealing with the ethical ramifications of referrals to ancillary businesses, the Florida Bar Association suggested that ancillary businesses must also comply with the Florida rules regarding solicitation.[369]

Consistent with its liberal treatment of ancillary businesses against the backdrop of referrals and advertising, the Boston Bar Association allows solicitation in certain circumstances. Although the bar follows the ABA Model Rules and prohibits lawyers engaged in law-related businesses from soliciting clients to their law firms, the Boston Bar Association does not attach the same ethical obligations to the ancillary business.[370] Therefore, it is quite possible in this area, too, that lawyers and nonlawyers engaged in a law-related business may solicit customers for the ancillary business without violating Rule 7.3.

Because comment 10 to Model Rule 5.7 implicates Model Rule 7.3 regarding solicitation as applying to law-related businesses, a labor law firm cannot solicit customers for its ancillary persuader firm in most jurisdictions. It may be possible, however, that a particular jurisdiction's bar would take a more flexible approach, like the Boston Bar Association suggests, and allow solicitation for the law-related business, though clearly not for the law firm itself. Even so, there seems to be no compelling reason to avoid running afoul of the jurisdiction's lawyer rules on marketing even in the context of the ancillary entity.

III. Analysis, Checklist for Compliance, and Conclusion

If the Obama administration narrows the definition of the advice exception built into the Labor Management Reporting and Disclosure Act, labor law firms may endeavor to establish ancillary consulting firms in order to offer clients the necessary persuader services without disclosing the names and receipts of their clients. Persuader services, such as drafting and revising union/management campaign materials, will likely fall within the ambit of the Rule 5.7 definition of law-related services. This is because attorneys would provide such services in conjunction with legal services, and the drafting and revising campaign materials do not constitute the unauthorized practice of law when rendered by nonlawyers.

As such, the persuader firm would very likely need to inform its customers that its services are not legal services and the attorney-client protections would not apply to any services rendered. Notwithstanding such a disclosure, the attorneys should be mindful that ethical obligations could extend to their ancillary business.

---

interpreting and reviewing them also apply to what might be seen as the soliciting acts of the ancillary wing.

[368] Ethics Digest, *Mediation: Responsibility Regarding Nonlegal Services*, 19 Penn. Lawyer 41, 41 (1997).
[369] *Annual Reports of Committees of the Florida Bar*, 79 Fla. Bar J. 1, 27 (2005).
[370] *See generally* Boston Bar Association, *Ethics Opinion 199-B: Law-Related Services (LRS)*, 43 Boston Bar J. 16 (1999).

Many jurisdictions adopting Model Rule 5.7 take the position that ethical rules regarding confidentiality of information, referrals, and advertising and solicitation apply in equal force to the ancillary businesses of attorneys. It is likely that other state bars and courts newly considering the question in the future will share this view as well, extending their ethics rules for lawyers to any entity controlled by lawyers, even if it is not providing traditional legal services as such. Although a minority position well represented and supported by one local bar association may provide some impetus for treating the ancillary business in its own compartment for purposes of the rules for lawyers, those firms in other jurisdictions planning to open such a wing cannot count on other bar associations and reviewing courts to honor such compartmentalization.

A labor law firm and its persuader activity consulting firm must therefore take certain precautions to avoid violations of ethical rules. These actions should work out to be not only good ethical practice but good business and client relations as well.

> First, the consulting firm should not freely exchange information regarding its customers with the law firm unless the customers give written, informed consent.
>
> Second, the law firm must be very careful when referring its clients to the persuader firm. If the firm wishes to do so, it must fully at the very least disclose the terms of the referral to the client, advise the client to seek independent counsel regarding the transaction, and obtain informed consent in writing from the client. On the other hand, the persuader firm may refer customers to the law firm for legal services without running afoul of ethical rules, if it follows the mandates of conflict of interest rules relating to lawyers involved in business with clients.
>
> Third, the labor law firm should advertise its consulting firm in the same manner that it advertises the law firm. Therefore, the advertisement must not contain any misrepresentation of fact or law, nor contain any omission that makes the advertisement seriously misleading. Moreover, any paper or electronic communication promoting the ancillary business must contain the words, "advertising material" and also must contain the name and address of at least one attorney responsible for the communication. Other requirements and vetting procedures that a particular jurisdiction has implemented for lawyers should be considered to extent to the nonlawyer wing as well.
>
> Fourth, the ABA Model Rule regarding solicitation (Rule 7.3), and its state court equivalent in a particular jurisdiction, will likely apply to the persuader firm just as applies to the law firm. Thus, the persuader firm may not solicit clients within the definition of that activity except to the extent those limits may be unconstitutional under First Amendment judicial review. Regardless, there seems to be no compelling reason to evade the solicitation and marketing rules for lawyers even in the operation of the ancillary business, to the extent a specific bar or court might allow it. To the extent such ethics interpretations do hamper the effective marketing and operation of the related business, perhaps an

advisory opinion from the controlling jurisdiction's bar organization should be sought.

The recommendations above flow from the ethics opinions of jurisdictions interpreting and tailoring their rules to the literal reading of the ABA Model Rule 5.7 and the accompanying comments. At least one ethics opinion, rendered by the Boston Bar Association, has interpreted ABA Model Rule 5.7 much more liberally. A labor law firm establishing a persuader firm in a jurisdiction that has yet to treat the ancillary business model should consider writing the relevant state bar association to request an opinion regarding the ethical obligations stemming from the business arrangement. This consultation may be sought in order to comply fully with whatever rules might also apply to the other business—and perhaps even to leave open the possibility of more flexibility in the operation and promotion of the new business.

Chapter 6

Canary in a Coal Mine: How *Caperton v. A.T. Massey Coal Co.* Demonstrates the Need for Oxygen and Reform in State Supreme Courts

Elizabeth A. Adams

"A canary in a coal mine is an early warning of danger."[371]

During a fire or after an explosion in a coal mine, carbon monoxide—a deadly gas devoid of color, taste, or smell—can form underground.[372] Before the availability of modern detection devices, miners used canaries—especially sensitive to methane and carbon monoxide—to detect any dangerous gas build-ups.[373] After a fire or explosion, rescuers would descend into the coal mine carrying a canary in a small cage.[374] They knew their air supply was safe as long as the canary kept singing.[375]

Modern carbon monoxide detectors and monitors have rendered obsolete the use of a caged canary.[376] The ideology behind the practice, however, has become a popular idiomatic expression in the English language.[377] Political and business analysts use the idiom to describe a "harbinger of the future."[378] A singular event in an isolated area may not seem particularly noteworthy, but could offer the first concrete warning of a large, growing problem.[379]

---

[371] UsingEnglish.com, *Idioms*, Canary in a Coal Mine, *available at* http://www.usingenglish.com/reference/idioms/canary+in+a+coal+mine.html (last visited May 15, 2010).

[372] United States Department of Labor, Mine Safety & Health Administration (MSHA), A Pictorial Walk Through the 20th Century, *Canaries, available at* http://www.msha.gov/century/canary/canary.asp (last visited May 15, 2010) ("MSHA, *Canaries*").

[373] Wisegeek.com, *What Does It Mean to be a "Canary in a Coal Mine"?*, http://www.wisegeek.com/what-does-it-mean-to-be-a-canary-in-a-coal-mine.htm (last visited May 15, 2010) ("Wisegeek.com") and MSHA, *Canaries, supra* 2.

[374] MSHA, *Canaries*, http://www.msha.gov/century/canary/canary.asp.

[375] Wisegeek.com, *supra, What Does It Mean to be a "Canary in a Coal Mine"?*

[376] *Id.*

[377] *Id.*

[378] *Id.*

[379] *Id.* For example, in a political sense, "a country's delegation abruptly leaving a meeting could be described as a canary in a coal mine for future negotiations." *Id.* Additionally, large corporations may use a 'canary in a coal mine' approach by testing a particular strategy. *Id.* The parent company can analyze the feasibility of the strategy by testing it in one of its smaller companies, thereby either avoiding an imminent failure, or benefiting from a jump on competition. *Id.*

Judicial bias, or the appearance of bias, can be difficult to detect. Just as carbon monoxide lacks color, taste, or smell, rarely will a judge candidly admit his bias; moreover, often he is not even aware of his bias.[380] According to survey results, U.S. public perception of the "fairness and impartiality of the courts" is on the decline.[381] Recently, the failure of judges to recuse themselves "in cases in which [the judges'] impartiality appears to be in question" has given rise to much controversy.[382] As such, judicial recusal is now a "hot topic" among legal scholars, and the U.S. public and press.[383]

Just as dangerous gas build up in coal mines causes a canary to stop singing, thereby signaling danger to rescue workers, the 2009 United States Supreme Court decision in *Caperton v. A.T. Massey Coal Co.*[384] signals a build up of dangerous practices in state courts of last resort that need to be addressed. Recognizing that the states "may choose to 'adopt recusal standards more rigorous than due process requires,' " the Court nevertheless concluded

> [t]hat there is a serious risk of actual bias—based on objective and reasonable perceptions—when a person with a personal stake in a particular case had a significant and disproportionate influence in placing the judge on the case by raising funds or directing the judge's election campaign when the case was pending or imminent."[385]

There is much debate around whether the Supreme Court was the appropriate body to set recusal standards. Whether or not the Court was the best venue to deal with the "temptation to remedy public perception that justice can be bought with campaign contributions,"[386] states should heed the *Caperton* decision as an early signal of danger regarding public confidence in judicial impartiality. Justice Brent Benjamin of the West Virginia Supreme Court of Appeals ("W.V.S.C."), the state's highest court, has become the "canary in a coal mine" for all the states' courts of last resort with regard to judicial elections, campaign financing, and recusal standards.

This paper will discuss judicial ethics, impartiality, and bias in the state courts of last resort in the United States with regard to judicial selection and recusal. Section I will provide a brief discussion of the *Caperton* decision. Next, Section II will briefly discuss current methods for judicial selection and retention in the states' courts of last resort. Section III will discuss judicial recusal. Finally, in Section IV, I will offer

---

[380] *See* Penny J. White, *The Supreme Court, 2008 Term: Relinquished Responsibilities*, 123 Harv. L. Rev. 120, 126 (2009).

[381] Keith R. Fisher, *Education for Judicial Aspirants*, 43 Akron L. Rev. 163, 185-90 (2010). In particular, certain identifiable groups, such as African-Americans and Hispanics, perceive there is "different justice for rich than for the poor," and believe "judges are not fair and impartial." *Id.* at 186.

[382] Jeffrey T. Fiut, Comment, *Recusal and Recompense: Amending New York Recusal Law in Light of the Judicial Pay Raise Controversy*, 57 Buffalo L. Rev. 1597, 1598 & n.5 (2009).

[383] *Id.* at 1598.

[384] Caperton v. A.T. Massey Coal Co., ___ U.S. ___, 129 S. Ct. 2252 (2009).

[385] *Caperton*, 129 S. Ct. at 2267, 2263-64 (citations omitted).

[386] Terri R. Day, *Buying Justice: Caperton v. A.T. Massey: Campaign Dollars, Mandatory Recusal and Due Process*, 28 Miss. C. L. Rev. 359, 373 (2009).

several suggestions on how States can act to restore public perception of judicial impartiality in the wake of *Caperton*.

I. *Caperton v. A.T. Massey Coal Co.*, and Recusal Under the Due Process Clause of the Fourteenth Amendment

> "It is not merely of *some* importance but is of *fundamental* importance that justice should not only be done, but should manifestly and undoubtedly be seen to be done."[387]

A West Virginia jury awarded Hugh Caperton, Harman Development Corp., Harman Mining Corp., and Sovereign Coal ("Caperton") $50 million in compensatory and punitive damages after finding A.T. Massey Coal Co. and its affiliates ("Massey") liable for fraudulent misrepresentation, concealment, and tortious interference with existing contractual relations.[388] The jury verdict and award were handed down in August 2002.[389] Nearly two years later, in June 2004, the state trial court, finding that Massey "'intentionally acted in utter disregard of [Caperton's] rights and ultimately destroyed [Caperton's] businesses because, after conducting cost-benefit analyses, [Massey] concluded it was in its financial interest to do so,'" denied Massey's post-trial motions challenging the verdict and the $50 million damages award.[390] Nine months later, in March 2005, "the trial court denied Massey's motion for judgment as a matter of law."[391]

After the jury verdict, but before the appeal, Donald L. Blankenship, chairman, CEO and president of Massey—knowing the W.V.S.C. would consider the appeal in the case—became involved in the 2004 West Virginia (W.V.) judicial elections.[392] Blankenship threw his financial and political support behind attorney Brent Benjamin, who sought to replace W.V.S.C. Justice Warren McGraw.[393] Blankenship donated the $1,000 statutory maximum to Benjamin's campaign committee; additionally, Blankenship donated almost $2.5 million to a political organization formed under 26 U.S.C. § 527, "And For the Sake Of The Kids" ("ASK").[394] ASK opposed McGraw and supported Benjamin, and Blankenship's "donations accounted for more than two-thirds of the total funds [ASK] raised."[395] What is more, Blankenship also spent "over $500,000 on independent expenditures—for direct mailings and letters soliciting donations as well as television and newspaper advertisements—'to support . . . Benjamin.' "[396] Blankenship's total $3 million in

---

[387] Rex v. Sussex Justices, 1 King's Bench Reports 256, 259 (1924) (Lord Hewart, 1870-1943) (emphasis added).
[388] *Caperton*, 129 S. Ct. at 2257.
[389] *Caperton*, 129 S. Ct. at 2257.
[390] *Caperton*, 129 S. Ct. at 2257 (internal citation omitted).
[391] *Caperton*, 129 S. Ct. at 2257.
[392] *Caperton*, 129 S. Ct. at 2257.
[393] *Caperton*, 129 S. Ct. at 2257; *see also* Terri R. Day, *Buying Justice: Caperton v. A.T. Massey: Campaign Dollars, Mandatory Recusal and Due Process*, 28 Miss. C. L. Rev. 359, 360 (2009).
[394] *Caperton*, 129 S. Ct. at 2257.
[395] *Caperton*, 129 S. Ct. at 2257.
[396] *Caperton*, 129 S. Ct. at 2257 (internal citations omitted).

contributions to Benjamin's election "were more than the total amount spent by *all other* Benjamin supporters and three times the amount spent by Benjamin's *own* committee. . . . Blankenship spent $1 million more than the *total* amount spent by the campaign committees of *both* candidates combined."[397] Benjamin won the 2004 election.[398]

Benjamin had been elected and sworn in to the W.V.S.C. by the time Massey's appeal reached W.V.'s highest court.[399] Benjamin was part of the 3-2 majority that reversed the lower court's $50 million verdict against Massey.[400] Caperton sought rehearing, and both parties moved for recusal of three of the five W.V.S.C. justices.[401] In total, Caperton filed three separate motions to recuse Benjamin.[402] Caperton sought to disqualify Benjamin from hearing the Massey case "based on the appearance of bias created by . . . Blankenship's financial support to . . . Benjamin's campaign."[403] Benjamin refused all three motions to recuse himself, "because Caperton failed to establish actual bias."[404] Two other justices, however, granted the parties' motions to recuse.[405]

The U.S. Supreme Court agreed, in November 2008, to consider whether the Due Process Clause of the Fourteenth Amendment required Benjamin to recuse himself in the *Caperton* case given Blankenship's financial support of Benjamin's election campaign.[406] Oral arguments took place March 3, 2009, and on June 8, 2009, the Court ruled in favor of Caperton in a 5-4 decision. In the majority opinion, which emphasized preserving the integrity of the judicial system, Justice Kennedy discussed how the Due Process Clause had previously been used to "mandate recusal in two situations: where a judge was found to have a financial interest in the case, and where a judge had participated in an earlier proceeding and was subsequently asked

---

[397] *Caperton*, 129 S. Ct. at 2257 (internal citations omitted) (emphasis added).
[398] *See Caperton*, 129 S. Ct. at 2257. Benjamin received 382,036 votes (53.3%), and McGraw received 334,301 votes (46.7%). *Id.*
[399] *Caperton*, 129 S. Ct. at 2257-58; *see also* Day, 28 Miss. C. L. Rev. at 360.
[400] *Caperton*, 129 S. Ct. at 2258. Although the state court majority found "'Massey's conduct warranted the type of judgment rendered in this case," it reversed. *Id.* (describing state court result). The W.V.S.C. based its reversal on two grounds. First, it held that a forum-selection clause contained in a contract (to which Massey was not a party) barred the suit in the state. *Id.* The second ground for reversal was that *res judicata* was found to bar the suit due to an out-of-state judgment (to which again Massey was not a party). *Id.*
[401] *Caperton*, 129 S. Ct. at 2258.
[402] Day, 28 Miss. C. L. Rev. at 360, *citing Brief for Respondents* at 8, *Caperton*, 129 S. Ct. 2252 (No. 08-22).
[403] Day, 28 Miss. C. L. Rev. at 360, *citing Brief for Respondents* at 8, *Caperton*, 129 S. Ct. 2252 (No. 08-22).
[404] Day, 28 Miss. C. L. Rev. at 360, *citing Brief for Respondents* at 8, *Caperton*, 129 S. Ct. 2252 (No. 08-22).
[405] *Caperton*, 129 S. Ct. at 2258. Photos surfaced of Justice Maynard vacationing with Blankenship in the French Riviera while the case was still pending; Maynard granted Caperton's recusal motion. *Id.* Justice Starcher granted Massey's recusal motion, based upon Starcher's public criticism of Blankenship's role in the 2004 judicial elections. *Id.* In Starcher's recusal memorandum he urged Benjamin to recuse himself as well. *Id.*
[406] Day, 28 Miss. C. L. Rev. at 361.

to determine the propriety of [his] actions in a later proceeding."[407] Holding that the present case created a third situation where due process mandated disqualification, the Court noted that due process did not require a consideration as to whether Benjamin was *actually* biased, but "due process requires an objective inquiry into whether the contributor's influence on the election under all the circumstances 'would offer a possible temptation to the average . . . judge to . . . lead him to not hold the balance nice, clear, and true.' "[408] Focusing on the fact that the justice system must not only be fair, it must also appear to be fair, the majority evaluated the circumstances from various points of view to take into account the perceptions of the parties, the lawyers, the judge, and the general public.[409] The majority decided the way a judicial action appears to "an objective outsider is more important than whether the judge personally believes [he] can be impartial."[410] As such, even if the decision is legally valid, and the judge is not actually biased, the majority regarded a decision given "by an apparently biased judge [as] unacceptable."[411]

The dissenting justices wrote that the majority opinion was too broad and unworkable, leaving too many uncertainties for judges and litigants.[412] Believing the Court "unfairly expects judges to be political scientists, economists, and psychologists," the dissenters perceived judges to be "at the mercy of unscrupulous lawyers, described by Justice Scalia as playing the litigation 'game' by 'contesting nonrecusal decisions through every available means.' "[413] In addition to taking a pejorative view of lawyers as trying to game the system, and judges as unsophisticated or needing bright line rules to withstand the unethical lawyers, the dissent pays most attention to how recusal motions will affect the individual judge.[414] The dissenters worried about whether a judge's reputation, and whether she will be able to defend herself, thereby considering "a recusal motion based on probable bias to be an affront to judicial dignity," writes one commentator.[415] Moreover, in his dissent, Chief Justice Roberts included a non-exhaustive list of forty "fundamental" questions he believed the majority's "probability of bias" and "debt of gratitude" opinion would leave for courts to have to determine on their own without "clear, workable guidance."[416]

---

[407] Jeffrey T. Fiut, Comment, *Recusal and Recompense: Amending New York Recusal Law in Light of the Judicial Pay Raise Controversy*, 57 Buffalo L. Rev. 1597, 1608 (2009), *citing Caperton*, 129 S. Ct. at 2263.
[408] *See* Fiut, 57 Buffalo L. Rev. at 1608, *citing Caperton*, 129 S. Ct. at 2264 (quoting Tumey v. Ohio, 237 U.S. 510, 532 (1927)) (emphasis added).
[409] Penny J. White, *The Supreme Court, 2008 Term: Relinquished Responsibilities*, 123 Harv. L. Rev. 120, 136 (2009).
[410] White, *The Supreme Court, 2008 Term: Relinquished Responsibilities*, 123 Harv. L. Rev. at 136.
[411] White, 123 Harv. L. Rev. at 136.
[412] *Caperton*, 129 S. Ct. 2252, 2272 (2009) (Roberts, C.J., dissenting).
[413] White, *The Supreme Court, 2008 Term: Relinquished Responsibilities*, 123 Harv. L. Rev. at 130, *citing Caperton*, 129 S. Ct. at 2272 (Roberts, C.J., dissenting), and 2274 (Scalia, J., dissenting).
[414] *See* White, 123 Harv. L. Rev. at 130, 137.
[415] White, 123 Harv. L. Rev. at 137.
[416] *Caperton*, 129 S. Ct. at 2269-2272 (Roberts, C.J., dissenting). For an excellent response to each of Chief Justice Roberts' forty questions, see Penny J. White, *The Supreme Court, 2008 Term: Relinquished Responsibilities*, 123 Harv. L. Rev. 120 (2009).

The majority's own guidelines as to when the Due Process Clause requires disqualification are: (1) "the contribution's relative size in comparison to the total amount of money contributed to the campaign," (2) "the total amount spent in the election," and (3) "the apparent effect such contribution had on the outcome of the election," while further, (4) "[t]he temporal relationship between the campaign contributions, the justice's election, and the pendency of the case is also critical."[417]

The Court reversed and remanded the case back to the W.V.S.C., requiring Benjamin to disqualify himself.[418] The W.V.S.C., even in the absence of Benjamin, ruled in favor of Massey in a 4-1 decision, focusing on the forum selection argument rather than the res judicata issue.[419] In a scathing dissent, Justice Workman pointed out, "Neither the sheer length of the majority's opinion [approximately sixty pages], nor the large number of cases cited (but erroneously applied), nor even its expansive conclusory statements, can obfuscate its lack of sound legal reasoning and its result-driven approach."[420] Justice Workman further contended that the majority allows Massey to cling to the forum selection clauses of contracts with which Massey fraudulently interfered.[421] Nonetheless, at the end of the day, Massey won.

II. Laboratory of the States: Judicial Selection and Retention

> "The genius of the American form of government has always been that states can experiment with different policies and learn from each other."[422]

Although the Supreme Court has decided that the Due Process Clause requires recusal in an additional circumstance, many feel that the states are best situated to handle when, how, and under what circumstances to recuse. Before addressing recusal (in Section III below) it is important to understand how the states select and retain the justices of their courts of last resort. "It is one of the happy incidents of

---

[417] *Caperton*, 129 S. Ct. at 2264 (majority opinion).

[418] *Caperton*, 129 S. Ct. at 2267.

[419] *Caperton v. A.T. Massey Coal Co.*, 690 S.E.2d 322 (W. Va. 2009). "For the reasons stated in the body of this opinion, we reverse the judgment in this case and remand for the circuit court to enter an order dismissing this case against A.T. Massey Coal Company and its subsidiaries *with prejudice*. Reversed and remanded." *Id.* at 357 (emphasis added).

[420] *Caperton*, 690 S.E.2d at 357 (dissenting opinion).

[421] *Caperton*, 690 S.E.2d at 366. "Yet in its now successful effort to wreak corporate and personal financial ruin on the Harman Companies and Mr. Caperton, Massey embraces the contract and its forum-selection clause almost amorously. The majority encourages this behavior by callously allowing Massey to benefit from the contract it sought to destroy." *Id.* (citation omitted). *See also* Jeffrey W. Stempel, *Completing Caperton and Clarifying Common Sense Through Using the Right Standard for Constitutional Judicial Recusal*, 29 Rev. Litig. 249, 259 n.37 (2010) ("Cynics might be forgiven for concluding that the [W.V.S.C.'s] resolute adherence to its earlier forum selection clause ruling was perhaps motivated by defensiveness about the U.S. Supreme Court's disqualification of Justice Benjamin and implicit indictment of the West Virginia Court's recusal practices.").

[422] Douglas Holtz-Eakin & Lawrence Mone, Manhattan Institute for Policy Research, *Use States As Health Care Reform Labs* (Feb. 26, 2010), *available at* http://www.manhattan-institute.org/html/miarticle.htm?id=5996 (last visited May 15, 2010).

the federal system that a single courageous State may, if its citizens choose, serve as a laboratory; and try novel social and economic experiments without risk to the rest of the country.'"[423] As such, that diversity could be seen as positive; "'[d]iversity not only in policy, but in the means of implementing policy, is the very *raison d'etre* of our federal system.'"[424]

Currently, "eighty-seven percent of state court judges face elections, and thirty-nine states elect at least some of their judges."[425] In the United States, more than seventy-five percent of the states have some form of judicial elections, although how the judges are elected differs among the states.[426] Although it is beyond the scope of this paper to address in great detail the history of judicial elections in the U.S., it is important to know a little about that history.

Anti-Federalists contended that "judicial elections would serve as a 'democratic check on judicial actions.' "[427] Alexander Hamilton and the Federalists posited that judicial independence "required life-time appointment for judges."[428] The Framers assumed that states would adopt a method of selecting judges congruous to the method laid out in the U.S. Constitution, namely that judges are appointed by the Executive "with the Advice and Consent of the Senate."[429] In fact, during the first fifty years of the U.S., the other branches of government appointed all state and federal judges.[430]

Judicial elections gained in popularity in the mid-nineteenth century.[431] Many attribute the rise of judicial elections to President Andrew Jackson and the "'Jacksonian movement toward greater popular control of public office.'"[432] In the mid- to late-nineteenth century, many supported judicial elections "believing popular validation from the polls would rebalance growing legislative and executive branch power."[433] In the mid-twentieth century, the struggle between those who perceived a loss in judicial independence and appearance of impartiality and those who sought to

---

[423] Brief of the States of Alabama, Colorado, Delaware, Florida, Louisiana, Michigan, and Utah as Amici Curiae Supporting Respondents, Caperton v. A.T. Massey Coal Co., 129 S. Ct. 2252 (2009) (No. 08-22), *quoting* New State Ice Co. v. Liebmann, 285 U.S. 262, 311 (1932) (Brandeis, J., dissenting).
[424] Brief of the States of Alabama, et al. as Amici Curiae in Supporting Respondents, *Caperton*, 129 S. Ct. 2252 (No. 08-22), *quoting* Harmelin v. Michigan, 501 U.S. 957, 990 (1991) (Scalia, J. concurring).
[425] Day, 28 Miss. C.L. Rev. at 364, *quoting* Adam Liptak, *Rendering Justice with One Eye on Re-election*, N.Y. Times, May 25, 2008, *available at* http://www.nytimes.com/2008/05/25/us/25exception.html (last visited May 15, 2010).
[426] Day, 28 Miss. C.L. Rev. at 364.
[427] *Id.* (citation omitted).
[428] *Id.*
[429] Jason D. Grimes, Note, *Aligning Judicial Elections with Our Constitutional Values: The Separation of Powers, Judicial Free Speech, and Due Process*, 57 Clev. St. L. Rev. 863, 868 (2009), *citing* U.S. Const. art. II, § 2, cl. 2.
[430] Grimes, 57 Clev. St. L. Rev. at 868.
[431] Day, 28 Miss. C.L. Rev. at 363.
[432] *Id.* at 364, *quoting* Republican Party of Minn. v. White, 536 U.S. 765, 791 (2002).
[433] Grimes, 57 Clev. St. L. Rev. at 869.

ensure judges would not "legislate from the bench" but would remain accountable to the people came together in the so-called Missouri Plan.

A. Missouri Plan: A Different Sort of Missouri Compromise

In the period between the two World Wars, Missouri voters grew disillusioned and "dissatisfied by the increasing role of politics in judicial selection and judicial decision-making."[434] Voters amended the Missouri constitution in 1940 by adopting the "Nonpartisan Selection of Judges Court Plan" (the "Missouri Plan").[435] A national model for the selection of judges, the Missouri Plan has been adopted in more than thirty other states.[436]

Under the Missouri Plan, judges are selected based on merit rather than political affiliation. Lawyers who wish to join the court submit their applications to a nonpartisan judicial commission. The members of the commission may vary depending upon the court, but the commission is usually a combination of peer-elected lawyers, and citizens appointed by the Governor; for example, for both the Missouri Supreme Court and the Missouri Court of Appeals, the Appellate Judicial Commission ("AJC") makes the selection. The AJC is a seven-member commission, composed of three citizens selected by the Governor, three lawyers elected by the lawyers of the Missouri bar, and the Supreme Court's Chief Justice, who serves as chair. Regardless of which commission handles the applications, the constitutional process of filling a judicial vacancy in Missouri is the same. After the nonpartisan judicial commission has reviewed applications and interviewed applicants, the commission then submits the names of three qualified candidates—called the "panel" of candidates—to the Missouri Governor. After interviewing candidates, the Governor then selects a member of the judicial "panel" to fill the vacancy.

Voters have a voice in the retention of judges under the Missouri Plan. In Missouri, after a judge has served in office for at least one year (the length of time may vary in other states), she must stand for a retention election at the next general election. In order to maintain the nonpartisan approach to filling the bench, the judge's name is placed on a separate judicial ballot, without political party designation. Missouri voters then decide whether to retain a judge based on his or her judicial record. Like the multi-member commissions used to select the judicial "panel," Missouri uses judicial performance evaluation committees ("JPECs")—comprised of lawyers and non-lawyers—to inform voters about the performance of nonpartisan judges. JPECs evaluate objective criteria of judges on the retention ballot, including surveys completed by lawyers and jurors who have direct and personal knowledge of the judges, as well as decisions written by the judges. The judicial performance standards used in rating judges' performances include whether he: "administer[s] justice impartially and uniformly; make[s] decisions based on competent legal

---

[434] Your Missouri Courts, *Missouri Nonpartisan Court Plan*, http://www.courts.mo.gov/page.jsp?id=297 (last visited May 15, 2010).

[435] Your Missouri Courts, *Missouri Nonpartisan Court Plan*, http://www.courts.mo.gov/page.jsp?id=297 (last visited May 15, 2010) (hereinafter cited as "Missouri Plan").

[436] *See Missouri Plan, supra*. All of the facts and quotes in the next three paragraphs are from the above-cited website, and to be clear I have not added individual footnotes for each fact. It is an informative website that touts the plan as a good one for other states to consider.

analysis and proper application of the law; issue[s] rulings and decisions that can be understood clearly; effectively and efficiently manage[s] [his] courtroom[ ] and the administrative duties of [his] office, including whether [he] issue[s] decisions promptly; and act[s] ethically and with dignity, integrity and patience."[437] JPECs distribute the results of these judicial performance evaluations to the public via the League of Women Voters, the media, and the internet.

In order to be retained for a full term of office, a judge must receive a majority of votes. The primary purpose of the "vote is to provide another accountability mechanism of the nonpartisan plan to ensure quality judges."[438] Should a judge resign or retire during or at the end of his or her term, a vacancy is then created. The new judge will fill the vacancy, obtaining his or her position under the previously described Missouri Plan. It has been seventy years since Missouri voters—outraged by the "political control" of ward bosses in St. Louis, and the "widespread abuses of the judicial system" by the "Boss Tom" Pendergast "political machine" in Kansas City—placed the Missouri Plan on the ballot by initiative petition.[439] The Missouri Plan appears to be successful in "selecting qualified judges" because, since its adoption, the public has not voted out any appellate judge; moreover, only two circuit judges have been voted out of office in seventy years.[440]

B. Other States

Many states have adopted the Missouri Plan, or a variation, but others continue to employ alternative methods. The systems for selecting judges of the highest courts of each state could of course be grouped into two main categories: elected versus appointed. Within those main categories, there are distinct subcategories. For example, states use partisan elections, nonpartisan elections, and partisan primaries followed by nonpartisan elections to select judges.[441]

With regard to appointment, some states use the Missouri Plan, employing a judicial nominating commission ("JNC") that provides a short list to the Governor, who in turn appoints the judge.[442] Other states allow the Governor to appoint, but the appointment is subject to confirmation from the JNC or its functional equivalent.[443] Similar to federal judges, some states require the Governor to appoint high court

---

[437] *Missouri Plan, supra.*
[438] *Id.*
[439] *Id.*
[440] *Id.* Judge Marion D. Waltner of Jackson County was voted out in 1942. *Id.* The other, Judge John R. Hutcherson of Clay County, was voted out in 1992 after receiving failing reviews from lawyers in the judicial evaluation survey. *Id.*
[441] Brief of the States of Alabama, et al. as Amici Curiae in Supporting Respondents, *Caperton*, 129 S. Ct. 2252 (No. 08-22), *supra, citing* American Judicature Society, *Methods of Judicial Selection*, http://www.judicialselection.us/judicial_selection/methods/selection_of_judges.cfm?state (last visited May 15, 2010) ("AJS, *Methods of Judicial Selection*").
[442] Brief of the States of Alabama, et al. as Amici Curiae in Supporting Respondents, *Caperton*, 129 S. Ct. 2252 (No. 08-22), *citing* AJS, *Methods of Judicial Selection*.
[443] Brief of the States of Alabama, et al. as Amici Curiae in Supporting Respondents, *Caperton*, 129 S. Ct. 2252 (No. 08-22), *citing* AJS, *Methods of Judicial Selection*.

justices subject to senate confirmation.[444] Still other states allow the Governor to appoint from a list created by the JNC; the appointment is subject to senate approval. One state requires the Governor to appoint from the recommendations of the JNC; such appointment is subject to approval from *both* of the legislative houses. In yet another state, the Governor nominates from recommendations by the JNC, and an "executive council"—a five-member body separately elected every two years through partisan elections—then formally makes her appointment. Finally, in two states, the legislature makes the selections.[445]

Given the diversity in selection of the judges throughout the states, it is not surprising that retention is equally diverse. Justices on the highest courts of each state are retained through reelection, retention vote, and selection by the Governor, which, in turn is followed by reappointment or reconfirmation by the appropriate body (e.g., senate, executive council, legislature, etc.).[446]

If judicial elections are "here to stay," as many believe they are, it is my opinion that those states that currently use either partisan or nonpartisan elections should switch to the Missouri Plan. The Missouri Plan allows for the "best of both worlds": restoration of appearance of fairness and impartiality through JNC recommendations, followed by gubernatorial appointment, and public participation to ensure accountability via a retention vote. More importantly, the public perception of the courts as "simply another political player"[447] could be ameliorated.

III: Are You Recusing Me?

> "Judges are the weakest link in our system of justice, and they are also the most protected."[448]

Although a complete history of judicial recusal is beyond the scope of this paper, a look at the history of recusal in the U.S. is necessary to understand the current state of disqualification. Under the first federal recusal law, codified in 1792, district court judges were required to disqualify themselves "in cases in which they had an interest as well as in cases where they were previously counsel to a party now appearing" before them.[449] Early in the nineteenth century, but before the first judicial election,

---

[444] Brief of the States of Alabama, et al. as Amici Curiae in Supporting Respondents, *Caperton*, 129 S. Ct. 2252 (No. 08-22), *citing* AJS, *Methods of Judicial Selection*.

[445] Brief of the States of Alabama, et al. as Amici Curiae in Supporting Respondents, *Caperton*, 129 S. Ct. 2252 (No. 08-22), *citing* AJS, *Methods of Judicial Selection*.

[446] Brief of the States of Alabama, et al. as Amici Curiae in Supporting Respondents, *Caperton*, 129 S. Ct. 2252 (No. 08-22), *citing* AJS, *Methods of Judicial Selection*.

[447] Ronald M. George, *The Supreme Court of California 2007-2008: Foreword: Achieving Impartiality in State Courts*, 97 Calif. L. Rev. 1853, 1857 (2009); *see also* Lawrence Lessig, *The Supreme Court, 2008 Term: What Everybody Knows and What Too Few Accept*, 123 Harv. L. Rev. 104, 110-11 (2009) (judiciary is to be that one sphere insulated from the relevance of money to the decision).

[448] Alan M. Dershowitz, Professor, Harvard Law School, *quoted in* Jerrold K. Footlick & Phyllis Malamud, *A Man for All Cases*, Newsweek, Feb. 20, 1978.

[449] Jeffrey T. Fiut, Comment, *Recusal and Recompense: Amending New York Recusal Law in Light of the Judicial Pay Raise Controversy*, 57 Buffalo L. Rev. 1597, 1602 (2009).

"recusal was broadened to include 'all judicial relationship or connection with a party that would in the judge's opinion make it improper to sit.'"[450]

Fast-forward to the twentieth century: in 1911, federal law required district court judges to disqualify themselves for bias, and in 1948, the 1911 law was not only broadened in its terms, but also applied to all federal judges.[451] Although these developments were vast improvements on recusal, the standards were still subjective. Fueled by the social climate of the late 1960s and early 1970s—most notably, the Civil Rights Movement, the Vietnam War, and the Watergate scandal—the public demanded increased accountability and greater transparency from the government. Against that backdrop, both the ABA and the Supreme Court criticized the subjective standard of the applicable statute, 28 U.S.C § 455.[452] In the alliterative *Commonwealth Coatings Corp. v. Continental Casualty Co.*,[453] the Court cautioned a court to avoid any action that "'may reasonably tend to awaken the suspicion' " that the judge's personal or business relations could be considered "'an element in influencing his judicial conduct.'"[454]

In late June 1972, just a few days after five men, one of whom claimed he used to work for the CIA, were arrested trying to bug the offices of the Democratic National Committee at the Watergate hotel and office complex, the Court handed down its decision in *Laird v. Tatum*.[455] In *Laird*, a civil liberties action was brought against the United States Army for (none other than) unlawful surveillance.[456] Justice William Rehnquist refused to disqualify himself, despite having testified about the alleged unlawful surveillance "as Assistant Attorney General while the appeal was pending."[457] Not only did Justice Rehnquist refuse to disqualify himself, but, like Benjamin, he cast the deciding vote in a controversial case.[458]

The *Laird* case and Watergate were not the only major events in 1972 with regard to the ethics of government officials. The ABA weighed in on ethics in the judiciary that year. As one scholar describes it, "Canon 3(C)(1) of the 1972 [ABA] Code of Judicial Conduct ushered in an entirely new standard for deciding when a judge should recuse [himself].... [T]he Code provided that 'a judge should disqualify himself in a proceeding in which his impartiality might reasonably be questioned.' This language required a judge to view the situation from the perspective of a disinterested party

---

[450] Fiut, 57 Buffalo L. Rev. at 1602, *quoting* Liteky v. United States, 510 U.S. 540, 544 (1994) (giving history of federal recusal laws).
[451] Fiut, 57 Buffalo L. Rev. at 1603. "Any justice or judge in the United States shall disqualify himself in any case in which he has substantial interest, has been of counsel, is or has been a material witness, or is so related to or connected with any party or his attorney as to render it improper, in his opinion, for him to sit on the trial, appeal, or other proceeding therein." *Id.*, *quoting* 28 U.S.C. § 455 (1970).
[452] Fiut, 57 Buffalo L. Rev. at 1603.
[453] 393 U.S. 145 (1968).
[454] Fiut, 57 Buffalo L. Rev. at 1603-04, *quoting* Commonwealth Coatings Corp. v. Continental Casualty Co. 393 U.S. 145, 150 (1968).
[455] 408 U.S. 1 (1972).
[456] *See* Fiut, 57 Buffalo L. Rev. at 1604.
[457] Fiut, 57 Buffalo L. Rev. at 1604.
[458] *Id.*

and determine whether it appeared [his] impartiality might be in doubt."[459] After the ABA adopted the objective recusal standard in 1972, Congress followed suit in 1974, amending § 455.[460]

Because a judge could be his "own arbiter as to whether [his] interest" would warrant recusal, Congress "overhauled" the law by creating two separate recusal provisions.[461] Congress co-opted language from the ABA Code, and created a new and broader category of recusal. Under § 455(a) of the statute, federal law now required a judge to use an objective standard in determining whether to disqualify himself. Additionally, § 455(a) replaced a "bias-in-fact" standard with an "appearance-of-bias" standard.[462] It is not relevant whether the bias was not factually exhibited under the "appearance of bias" standard. Under this standard, a judge is required to disqualify himself "merely if it appears [h]e might be biased."[463]

Under § 455(b), the areas of compulsory recusal, which require recusal in certain situations regardless of how disinterested the judge may be, were retained.[464] Recusal is currently mandatory in a variety of situations:

> (1) Where he [the judge] has a personal bias or prejudice concerning a party, or personal knowledge of disputed evidentiary facts concerning the proceeding; (2) Where in private practice he served as lawyer in the matter in controversy, or a lawyer with whom he previously practiced law served during such association as a lawyer concerning the matter, or the judge or such lawyer has been a material witness concerning it; (3) Where he has served in governmental employment and in such capacity participated as counsel, adviser or material witness concerning the proceeding or expressed an opinion concerning the merits of the particular case in controversy; (4) He knows that he, individually or as a fiduciary, or his spouse or minor child residing in his household, has a financial interest in the subject matter in controversy or in a party to the proceeding, or any other interest that could be substantially affected by the outcome of the proceeding; (5) He or his spouse, or a person within the third degree of relationship to either of them, or the spouse of such a person: (i) Is a party to the proceeding, or an officer, director, or trustee of a party; (ii) Is acting as a lawyer in the proceeding; (iii) Is known by the judge to have an interest that could be substantially affected by the outcome of the proceeding; (iv) Is to the judge's knowledge likely to be a material witness in the proceeding.[465]

In addition to recusal under federal law and state judicial codes, guidance for recusal can also be found in the Due Process Clause of the Fifth and Fourteenth Amendments,[466] as seen above in Section I.

---

[459] *Id.* (citation omitted).
[460] *Id.* at 1605.
[461] *Id.*
[462] *Id.* at 1605-06.
[463] *Id.* at 1606.
[464] *Id.* at 1605.
[465] 28 U.S.C. § 455(b) (2006).
[466] Fiut, 57 Buffalo L. Rev. at 1607.

Almost every state has adopted the most recent ABA Code of Judicial Conduct, namely Canon 2, "A judge shall avoid impropriety and the appearance of impropriety.[467] Moreover, the ABA and state codes of conduct "serve to maintain the integrity of the judiciary and the rule of law.[468]

Just as the political histories, court systems, and judicial selection methods of the states vary, the states' recusal rules are not uniform.[469] States have had the freedom to regulate judicial bias—whether real or apparent—through bar codes, rules, and statutes.[470] The Due Process Clause has required recusal only in "the most extreme cases—namely, where a judge either has a pecuniary 'interest in the outcome of a case' or is 'actually bias[ed]' against one of the parties."[471] Because individual states are in a better position to regulate recusal practice in their own courts, and because states have been "both vigorous and innovative in doing so," some contend there is no "pressing need" to raise state recusal practice to a U.S. constitutional level.[472] As such, some believe that the *Caperton* decision was the Court's encroachment into territory best left to the states to police.[473]

According to some critics, then, recusal should not be federalized because it "has always been, and always will be, a highly contextualized issue."[474] "The recusal inquiry 'is an objective one, made from the perspective of a reasonable observer who is informed of all the surrounding facts and circumstances.' "[475] States have used various methods to ensure judicial fairness, including recusal codes and statutes; "peremptory recusal" rules; contribution limits; public financing; and contribution-based recusal rules.[476] Thus, some contend, states are best left to be laboratories of experimentation, allowed to come up with unique results tailored to the unique judicial climate of their particular state.

---

[467] *Caperton*, 129 S. Ct. at 2266, *quoting* ABA Annotated Model Code of Judicial Conduct, Canon 2 (2004).
[468] *Caperton*, 129 S. Ct. at 2266.
[469] *See* Brief of the States of Alabama, et al. as Amici Curiae in Supporting Respondents, *Caperton*, 129 S. Ct. 2252 (No. 08-22).
[470] Brief of the States of Alabama, et al. as Amici Curiae in Supporting Respondents, *Caperton*, 129 S. Ct. 2252 (No. 08-22).
[471] Brief of the States of Alabama, et al. as Amici Curiae in Supporting Respondents, *Caperton*, 129 S. Ct. 2252 (No. 08-22), *citing* Bracy v. Gramley, 520 U.S. 899, 904 (1997).
[472] Brief of the States of Alabama, et al. as Amici Curiae in Supporting Respondents, *Caperton*, 129 S. Ct. 2252 (No. 08-22).
[473] *See* Lessig, 123 Harv. L. Rev. at 112, 118 ("*Caperton* was a mistake. The Supreme Court was wrong to expand the reach of due process to remedy the bad judgment of this state supreme court justice because, paradoxically, its opinion too will likely, and unnecessarily, weaken respect for the judiciary.... [A]ctivisim by the Court can weaken the capacity of other institutions to do the work they are better designed to do.").
[474] Brief of the States of Alabama, et al. as Amici Curiae in Supporting Respondents, *Caperton*, 129 S. Ct. 2252 (No. 08-22).
[475] Brief of the States of Alabama, et al. as Amici Curiae in Supporting Respondents, *Caperton*, 129 S. Ct. 2252 (No. 08-22), *quoting* Microsoft Corp. v. United States, 530 U.S. 1301, 1301 (2000) (Rehnquist, C.J.).
[476] Brief of the States of Alabama, et al. as Amici Curiae in Supporting Respondents, *Caperton*, 129 S. Ct. 2252 (No. 08-22).

For example, following the 2004 judicial election, and the controversy surrounding Benjamin's non-recusal in the state *Caperton* case, West Virginia revised its "campaign finance laws related to judicial elections."[477] Seeking to further refine the laws regarding the judiciary and perceived or real bias, the West Virginia legislature, in 2008, proposed an amendment to the state's constitution.[478] The amendment would create a three-member "Judicial Review Commission," which would have the authority to issue "'binding decision[s] on whether a family court judge, a circuit court judge or a supreme court justice should be recused from hearing, deciding or participating in deciding,' " in a given case.[479]

The various states' recusal methods, however, have seemed to run out of oxygen. At least where campaign contributions are concerned, the U.S. Supreme Court decided it needed to rescue recusal. Because states are free to implement stricter standards than due process requires, the following section offers several suggestions for the twenty-first century and its politicized judicial climate. It is imperative that public confidence in the judicial system is revived.

IV: Actions to Restore Public Confidence

> "We must never forget that the only real source of power that we as judges can tap is the respect of the people."[480]

Approximately ninety-eight percent of disputes filed in U.S. courts are decided in state courts.[481] Whether to pay a traffic ticket or to obtain a copy of an official document, or "whether as a party, witness, juror or victim," members of the public are most likely to come into contact with state courts.[482] Because studies in recent decades have shown that public confidence in the independence of the judiciary is waning, and because via *Caperton* the Supreme Court decided to pump oxygen into a waning recusal system in at least one state, the following reforms should be considered.[483]

---

[477] Brief of the States of Alabama, et al. as Amici Curiae in Supporting Respondents, *Caperton*, 129 S. Ct. 2252 (No. 08-22), *citing* 2005 W. Va. Acts, Ch. 9. Under the amended law, §527 groups—such as ASK, into which Blankenship sunk $2.5 million dollars—are required to register and disclose their financing; additionally, the West Virginia law sets a $1000-per-election cap on individual contributions to §527 groups operating in the state. *Id.*, *citing* W. Va. Code §3-8-12.

[478] *See* Brief of the States of Alabama, et al. as Amici Curiae in Supporting Respondents, *Caperton*, 129 S. Ct. 2252 (No. 08-22) (describing state's ameliorative efforts).

[479] Brief of the States of Alabama, et al. as Amici Curiae in Supporting Respondents, *Caperton*, 129 S. Ct. 2252 (No. 08-22), *quoting* H.R. J. Res. No. 104, 78th Leg., 2d Sess. (W. Va. 2008).

[480] Justice Thurgood Marshall, *quoted in* Chicago Tribune, Aug. 15, 1981.

[481] Ronald M. George, *The Supreme Court of California 2007-2008: Foreword: Achieving Impartiality in State Courts*, 97 Calif. L. Rev. 1853, 1855 (2009).

[482] George, 97 Calif. L. Rev. at 1855.

[483] These reforms are in no way unique to the author, but are a compilation of several leading suggestions offered by legal scholars.

1. Move to a Missouri Plan Model of Judicial Selection in States that Currently Employ Partisan or Nonpartisan Elections. See Section II(A), above, for a discussion of the Missouri Plan model.

2. Independent Review of Recusal Motions Using Objective Standards by Neutral Third Parties. States that have not already done so need to codify objective standards for independent review of recusal motions. Additionally, a justice should not be allow to review his own recusal motion. Moreover, his peers on the court of last resort on which he sits should also not be allowed to decide on the recusal motion. An independent commission, similar to that of the JNC used in selecting a shortlist of candidates for vacancies, should be used to decide recusal motions.[484]

3. Reasoned Decision-Making and Precedent. In addition to using independent third party commissions to decide on recusal motions, the commission should give public, written reasons. Such written documentation would not only give reviewing courts material for review, but would also create sort of precedent that judges, lawyers, and the public can refer to when deciding whether to file a recusal motion.[485]

4. System for Replacing Disqualified Justices. If a justice has been disqualified, the states need a procedural and substantive method for ensuring that there will be sufficient votes for a case to be decided. Retired justices of the state's highest court, or judges from state courts of intermediary appeal, could be used in rotation or lottery or alphabetically to replace judges who have been recused.[486]

5. Judicial Education. Several civil law countries have special schools specifically for the training of judges and magistrates. While there is debate in the U.S. as to whether education should come in the form of an LL.M. program, a summer seminar, or a short week-long evening program, the House of Delegates of the ABA voted "overwhelmingly to approve a resolution and recommendation urging state high courts and state, local, and territorial bar associations to establish voluntary programs of Introductory Judicial Education."[487]

The states are in desperate need of restoring the public's confidence in the judiciary. Although far from an exhaustive list of the remedies for the breathing new life into the dying reputation of state courts, the above reforms are at least a starting point for

---

[484] *See* Jeffrey T. Fiut, Comment, *Recusal and Recompense: Amending New York Recusal Law in Light of the Judicial Pay Raise Controversy*, 57 Buffalo L. Rev. 1597 (2009).

[485] *See* Deborah Goldberg, James Sample & David E. Pozen, *The Best Defense: Why Elected Courts Should Lead Recusal Reform*, 46 Washburn L.J. 503, 531 (2007).

[486] *See id.* at 532; *see also* J. Timothy Eaton & Lynn A. Ellenberger, *When Recusal Leads to Deadlock: A Constitutional Cure: A Recent U.S. Supreme Court's Opinion May Increase the Number of Recusals in Illinois, Which Could Lead to Important Cases Not Being Decided by Our State's Highest Court*, 97 Illinois B. J. 510 (Oct. 1, 2009).

[487] Keith R. Fisher, *Education for Judicial Aspirants*, 43 Akron L. Rev. 163 (2010).

state legislatures.[488] Judicial elections are different from other elections, because the judiciary depends not only upon *actual* impartiality, but also on the *appearance* of impartiality.[489] As such, states that are using partisan and nonpartisan elections to select judges should move to the Missouri Plan.

Additionally, there must be objective standards for recusal: neutral, independent third party commissions must adjudicate recusal motions. Of course, states are free to experiment with exactly how to create their commissions, and what system to use for replacing judges who have been recused. All states, however, should heed the "canary in the coal mine" and realize that judicial ethics, judicial impartiality, and the appearance of judicial impartiality are in dire need of oxygen.

---

[488] *See* Pamela S. Karlan, *The Supreme Court, 2008 Term: Electing Judges, Judging Elections, and the Lessons of Caperton*, 123 Harv. L. Rev. 80, 100-01 (2009) ("Thus, if *Caperton* is to have a lasting impact, it will occur through either legislative change or changes in judicial culture rather than through litigation. *Caperton* can work only if it leads to ex ante recusals by judges rather than ex post reversals of judgments.").

[489] *See* Lawrence Lessig, *The Supreme Court, 2008 Term: What Everybody Knows and What Too Few Accept*, 123 Harv. L. Rev. 104, 109 (2009) ("We presume the integrity of the (federal) judical branch. We presume the corruption (in this limited but important sense) of the legislative branch. The difference is enormously important to the health and power of each: trust in the judicial branch has been steady and strong; trust in the legislative branch has been falling and weak.").

Chapter 7

Negotiation Ethics: Balancing Ethically Permissible Conduct with Integrity and Professionalism in Settlement Talks

Camalla Kimbrough

The number of cases that go to trial has decreased significantly over the last few decades.[490] Due to ever-expanding court dockets and increasing litigation costs,[491] among other reasons, most legal disputes today are resolved through settlement negotiations.[492] Settlement negotiations often take place in the absence of judicial supervision.[493] In fact, judges and courts rarely take part in settlement negotiations absent a claim of conduct that amounts to fraud.[494] Accordingly, because settlement negotiations constitute "nonpublic behavior," negotiators can, for the most part, rest assured that "there will be no trial, no public testimony by conflicting witnesses, and thus no opportunity to examine the truthfulness of assertions made during the negotiation."[495] Such assurances facilitate the creation of a less than truthful atmosphere in the context of settlement negotiations, since the likelihood of discovery and punishment is minimal at best.[496]

The American Bar Association's Model Rules of Professional Conduct ("Model Rules") provide only minimal guidance regarding the parameters of settlement negotiations.[497] Model Rule 4.1, entitled "Truthfulness in Statements to Others," broadly governs settlement negotiations.[498] Model Rule 4.1 will be discussed in more detail in Part I. For now, it is important to note that because the Model Rules are minimalist standards,[499] they lack clear guidance as to what behavior is appropriate in the negotiations context, even if such behavior does not run afoul of established ethical rules.

---

[490] Pat V. Tremmel, *Much Celebrated American Trial is Dying in Real Life*, Northwestern University Newscenter, Mar. 9, 2009, http://www.northwestern.edu/newscenter/stories/2009/03/burnstrial.html.
[491] Patrick McDermott, *Lying by Omission? A Suggestion for the Model Rules*, 22 Geo. J. Legal Ethics 1015, 1015 (2009).
[492] Gerald B. Wetlaufer, *The Ethics of Lying in Negotiations*, 75 Iowa L. Rev. 1219, 1220 (1990).
[493] Barry R. Temkin, *Misrepresentation by Omission in Settlement Negotiations: Should There Be a Silent Safe Harbor?*, 18 Geo. J. Legal Ethics 179, 182 (2004).
[494] Debra S. Katz & Julie Chambers, *Attorneys' Ethical Responsibilities During Settlement Negotiations*, available at http://files.ali-aba.org/thumbs/datastorage/skoobesruoc/pdf/22KatzSettlementNegotCG047_thumb.pdf.
[495] James J. White, *Machiavelli and the Bar: Ethical Limitations on Lying in Negotiation*, 1980 Am. B. Found. Res. J. 926, 926 (1980).
[496] *Id.*
[497] Temkin, *Misrepresentation by Omission*, 18 Geo. J. Legal Ethics at 182.
[498] *Id.* at 186.
[499] Benjamin H. Barton, *The ABA, The Rules, and Professionalism: The Mechanics of Self-Defeat and a Call For a Return to the Ethical, Moral, and Practical Approach of the Canons*, 83 N.C.L. Rev. 411, 421 (2005).

As a result of this deficiency in the Model Rules,[500] lawyers often experience tension between their dual duties of zealous advocacy, and candor and fair dealing with others.[501] The Preamble to the Model Rules states that as a negotiator, "a lawyer seeks a result advantageous to the client but consistent with the requirements of honest dealings with others."[502] However, the Model Rules themselves do not require truthfulness and fair dealing,[503] which has left many commentators to ponder over what behaviors are appropriate for settlement negotiations.

Commentators who endorse the late Judge Alvin B. Rubin's position believe that a lawyer "must act honestly and in good faith" and "may not accept a result that is unconscionably unfair to the other party."[504] Others commentators believe that deception is inherent in the practice of negotiating, and that a lawyer must take advantage of every opportunity that is within the bounds of the law to fulfill his duty of zealous advocacy.[505] Professor James J. White's position is often cited in support of this proposition: "[t]o conceal one's true position, to mislead an opponent about one's true settling point, is the essence of negotiation."[506]

Still other commentators adopt a middle ground approach, suggesting that lawyers must balance the duty of zealous advocacy with personal integrity and professionalism considerations.[507] As noted by Professor Eleanor Holmes Norton, "[in] negotiation, where there is only the sparsest written guidance, the parties must decide for themselves what is legal, what is factual, and what is ethical."[508] In this paper, I argue that complying with ethical rules should not end the discussion about what behavior is appropriate in settlement negotiations. Instead, one must also take into account personal integrity and professionalism considerations.

Part I will discuss Model Rule 4.1 along with three areas that are not directly addressed by this rule. Part II will discuss whether these areas should be addressed by the rules. Finally, Part III will examine my personal views on the areas not addressed by the rules, and what course of action I will take knowing that certain behaviors may not amount to ethical violations.

I. Model Rule 4.1 and Related Rules: Truthfulness in Statements to Others

The language of Model Rule 4.1 reads as follows:

> In the course of representing a client a lawyer shall not knowingly:
>
> (a) make a false statement of material fact or law to a third person, or

---

[500] Michael H. Rubin, *The Ethics of Negotiations: Are There Any?*, 56 La. L. Rev. 447, 456 (1995).
[501] *See* Temkin, 18 Geo. J. Legal Ethics at 184.
[502] American Bar Association, Model Rules of Professional Conduct: Preamble (2009).
[503] Michael H. Rubin, *The Ethics of Negotiations: Are There Any?*, 56 La. L. Rev. 447, 453 (1995).
[504] Alvin B. Rubin, *A Causerie on Lawyers' Ethics in Negotiation*, 35 La. L. Rev. 577, 589, 581 (1975).
[505] *See* ABA Comm. on Ethics and Prof'l Responsibility, Formal Op. 06-439 (2006).
[506] White, *Machiavelli and the Bar*, 1980 Am. B. Found. Res. J. at 928.
[507] ABA Comm. on Ethics and Prof'l Responsibility, Formal Op. 06-439 (2006).
[508] Eleanor H. Norton, *Bargaining and the Ethics of Process*, 64 N.Y.U. L. Rev. 493, 529 (1989).

(b) fail to disclose a material fact when disclosure is necessary to avoid assisting a criminal or fraudulent act by a client, unless disclosure is prohibited by Rule 1.6.[509]

There are, among others, three issues not directly addressed under Rule 4.1(b): (1) the duty to disclose relevant legal authority to opposing counsel; (2) the duty to disclose relevant facts when opposing counsel is operating under mistaken facts; and (3) determining when mere lack of disclosure becomes equivalent to an affirmative false statement which violates Rule 4.1(a).

A. Duty to Disclose Relevant Legal Authority to Opposing Counsel

Under Model Rule 3.3(a)(2), a lawyer must "disclose to the tribunal legal authority in the controlling jurisdiction known to the lawyer to be directly adverse to the position of the client and not disclosed by opposing counsel."[510] However, no such requirement applies to lawyers in the negotiations context. Lawyers have no affirmative duty to disclose material legal authority to opposing counsel in settlement negotiations by virtue of Comment 2 to Model Rule 4.1, which unambiguously states that the rule only applies to "statements of fact."[511]

Consequently, for example, a lawyer has no duty to correct an opposing counsel's mistaken belief that that his client's potential recovery is limited by a tort reform statute, when in fact the statute has been found to be unconstitutional.[512] Similarly, a lawyer has no duty to inform opposing counsel that the statute of limitations has run on a client's claim.[513]

The lack of a duty to disclose relevant legal authority stems from the premise that lawyers are obligated to conduct their own legal research.[514] Lawyers have no right to expect that opposing counsel will do their work for them.[515] Furthermore, because lawyers have a duty to zealously advocate for their clients, they are prohibited from voluntarily disclosing weaknesses in their clients' cases.[516] Consequently, absent "special relationships or express contractual or statutory duties," lawyers are not required to reveal relevant legal authority to opposing counsel under Model Rule 4.1(b).[517]

---

[509] ABA, Model Rules of Prof'l Conduct R. 4.1 (2009).
[510] Model Rules of Prof'l Conduct R. 3.3(2)(2) (2009).
[511] Model Rules of Prof'l Conduct R. 4.1 cmt. 2 (2009).
[512] Patrick E. Longan, *Ethics in Settlement Negotiations Forward*, 52 Mercer L. Rev. 807, 815-16 (2001).
[513] ABA Comm. on Ethics and Prof'l Responsibility, Formal Op. 97-387 (1994).
[514] Charles B. Craver, *Negotiation Ethics: How to be Deceptive Without Being Dishonest/How to Be Assertive Without Being Offensive*, 38 S. Tex. L. Rev. 713, 720 (1997).
[515] *Id.*
[516] *See* ABA Comm. on Ethics and Prof'l Responsibility, Formal Op. 375 (1993).
[517] Craver, *Negotiation Ethics*, 38 S. Tex. L. Rev. at 721.

B. Duty to Disclose When Opposing Counsel Is Operating Under Mistaken Facts

Model Rule 4.1(b) requires disclosure whenever "*necessary to avoid assisting a criminal or fraudulent act by a client.*"[518] This subsection plainly addresses a scenario "where a client's crime or fraud takes the form of a lie or misrepresentation."[519] However, the rule does not address the scenario where the client is not perpetrating a crime or fraud, but rather, where opposing counsel is simply operating under mistaken facts. Comment 1 to Model Rule 4.1 says that a lawyer must be truthful when dealing with third parties on a client's behalf, but generally "has no affirmative duty to inform an opposing party of relevant facts."[520] On the other hand, Model Rule 8.4 requires that a lawyer refrain from engaging in conduct "involving dishonesty, fraud deceit, or misrepresentation," or that "is prejudicial to the administration of justice."[521]

Although lacking the authority of black letter law, the *Ethical Guidelines for Settlement Negotiations*, drafted by the ABA Section of Litigation in 2002, provides informal guidance for lawyers seeking advice on ethical issues that might arise in settlement negotiations.[522] Regarding mistakes made by opposing counsel, Ethical Guideline 4.3.5 states that a lawyer "should not exploit an opposing party's material mistake of fact that was *induced by the lawyer or the lawyer's client* and, in such circumstances, may need to disclose information to the extent necessary to prevent the opposing party's reliance on the material mistake of fact."[523] The Committee Notes for Ethical Guideline 4.3.5 add:

> Although there is no general ethics obligation, in the settlement context or elsewhere, to correct the erroneous assumptions of the opposing party or opposing counsel, the duty to avoid misrepresentations and misleading implies a professional responsibility to correct mistakes induced by the lawyer or the lawyer's client and not to exploit such mistakes.[524]

This text specifically delineates a duty to correct opposing counsel's mistaken assumptions that have been induced by the lawyer. Such mistakes may arise when a lawyer makes a true but incomplete statement of facts.[525] The implied duty to correct the mistakes stems from the fact that the failure to correct such mistakes may become the equivalent of an overt misrepresentation, in violation of Model Rule 4.1(a).

However, it is important to note that not all partially true statements will constitute overt misrepresentations. Comment 2 of Model Rule 4.1 states that in some cases "certain types of statements ordinarily are not taken as statements of fact," including

---

[518] Model Rules of Prof'l Conduct R. 4.1 (2009) (emphasis added).
[519] Model Rules of Prof'l Conduct R. 4.1 cmt. 3 (2009).
[520] *Id.* cmt. 2.
[521] Model Rules of Prof'l Conduct R. 8.4 (2009).
[522] *See* Temkin, *Misrepresentation by Omission*, 18 Geo. J. Legal Ethics at 190 (discussing impact of ABA Ethical Guidelines).
[523] ABA Section of Litigation, Ethical Guidelines for Settlement Negotiations 56 (2002) (emphasis added).
[524] *Id.* at 56-57.
[525] Temkin, *Misrepresentation by Omission*, 18 Geo. J. Legal Ethics at 183.

"estimates of price or value placed on the subject of a transaction and a party's intentions as to an acceptable settlement of a claim."[526] Thus, puffing and embellishment are to be expected in settlement negotiations.[527] In addition, mere statements of opinion are excluded under Model Rule 4.1.[528]

Even where a lawyer is not responsible for opposing counsel's mistaken assumptions, she may have a duty to correct the mistake under some limited circumstances.[529] This is premised on the idea that there is "a general duty of fairness that trumps the adversary system of justice in general and the attorney's duty of zealous advocacy to clients in particular."[530] Thus, a lawyer many not knowingly exploit a scrivener's error (e.g., a typographical or mathematical error) in a draft of a settlement agreement.[531] The Committee Notes for Ethical Guideline 4.3.5 note that "it would be unprofessional, and possibly unethical" to knowingly take advantage of opposing counsel's drafting error.[532] In addition, ABA Formal Opinion 95-397 says that a lawyer must inform opposing counsel of the death of his client before accepting a pending settlement offer.[533]

Because the duty to correct a mistaken assumption not induced by the lawyer only applies in limited circumstances, a lawyer generally has no obligation to correct opposing counsel's mistaken assumptions. A lawyer "is not expected to be his . . . brother's keeper."[534] Thus, where opposing counsel uses "a valuation by purchase price of an asset when the market value is much higher," a lawyer has no duty to disclose this erroneous valuation.[535] However, a lawyer must be aware that a misrepresentation can occur if he "incorporates or affirms a statement of another person that the lawyer knows to be false."[536] Thus, although there may be no general duty to correct the mistaken assumptions of opposing counsel, a lawyer must be careful not to incorporate or affirm the mistaken assumptions, in order to comply with Model Rule 4.1(b).[537]

C. Distinguishing Between Mere Lack of Disclosure and Overt Misrepresentation

As discussed above, Comment 1 to Model Rule 4.1 says that a lawyer has no affirmative duty to disclose relevant facts to opposing counsel.[538] However, Comment 1 goes on to say that an omission of facts may be unethical if it amounts to an affirmative false statement.[539] Because the Model Rules do not expound on these

---

[526] Model Rules of Prof'l Conduct R. 4.1 cmt. 2 (2009).
[527] Craver, *Negotiation Ethics*, 38 S. Tex. L. Rev. at 726.
[528] *Id.* at 727.
[529] ABA Section of Litigation, Ethical Guidelines for Settlement Negotiations 57 (2002).
[530] Temkin, *Misrepresentation by Omission*, 18 Geo. J. Legal Ethics at 181.
[531] Patrick E. Longan, *Ethics in Settlement Negotiations Forward*, 52 Mercer L. Rev. 807, 814-15 (2001).
[532] ABA Section of Litigation, Ethical Guidelines for Settlement Negotiations 57 (2002).
[533] ABA Comm. on Ethics and Prof'l Responsibility, Formal Op. 97-397 (1995).
[534] Longan, 52 Mercer L. Rev. at 815.
[535] *Id.* at 814-15.
[536] Model Rules of Prof'l Conduct R. 4.1 cmt. 1 (2009).
[537] Craver, *Negotiation Ethics*, 38 S. Tex. L. Rev. at 724.
[538] Model Rules of Prof'l Conduct R. 4.1 cmt. 1 (2009).
[539] *Id.*

seemingly contradictory statements, "it is unclear at what point the choice to withhold certain facts becomes an omission equivalent to a false affirmative statement."[540]

For example, according to the language of Model Rule 4.1(b), a lawyer's ethical duty of confidentiality trumps his ethical duty of disclosure.[541] Consequently, absent client consent or except under limited circumstances, a lawyer may not disclose information protected by Rule 1.6.[542] Thus, in Formal Opinion 375, the ABA concluded that although a lawyer knew pertinent information regarding the defrauding of a government bank examiner, the lawyer could not reveal this information pursuant to his duty of client confidentiality.[543] In such circumstances, a lawyer may be required to withdraw representation under Model Rule 1.16 in order to avoid aiding the client in perpetrating a crime or fraud.[544]

Nevertheless, a lawyer may have a duty to disclose information in certain circumstances even if it is not necessary to prevent a client from perpetrating a crime or fraud (e.g., drafting errors discussed above), and even when such a disclosure would likely violate Model Rule 1.6 (e.g., death of a client). This is premised on "intuitive notions of fairness."[545] Consequently, the Model Rules do not provide a bright line rule as to when it is acceptable to not disclose information, and when a failure to disclose becomes the equivalent of an overt misrepresentation that is punishable under Model Rule 4.1(a).

II. Whether These Areas Should Be Included in the Model Rules

Given that the aforementioned areas are not explicitly addressed under Model Rule 4.1(b), the question becomes whether these areas should be included in the Model Rules. In my opinion, the absence of a duty to disclose relevant legal authority to opposing counsel should be explicitly provided for in the rules; they should confirm and support the practice that a lawyer has no such duty as to misunderstandings of law. A lawyer's general duty is to his client and not to the opposing party: she must "secure and protect the client's legal rights and benefits" and "use legal procedures, within the limits of the law, to the fullest benefit of the client's cause."[546] A lawyer has no right to expect that his adversary will aid him in this cause, whether by pointing out legal authority which supports his client's position, or legal authority which weakens his adversary's position. Given that this appears to be a common practice rule, I see no reason why it should not be explicitly incorporated into black letter law.

---

[540] McDermott, *Lying by Omission?*, 22 Geo. J. Legal Ethics at 1021.
[541] ABA Section of Litigation, Ethical Guidelines for Settlement Negotiations 38 (2002).
[542] *See* Model Rules of Prof'l Conduct R. 1.6 (2009).
[543] ABA Comm. on Ethics and Prof'l Responsibility, Formal Op. 375 (1993).
[544] Debra S. Katz & Julie Chambers, *Attorneys' Ethical Responsibilities During Settlement Negotiations*, *available at* http://files.ali-aba.org/thumbs/datastorage/skoobesruoc/pdf/22KatzSettlementNegotCG047_thumb.pdf.
[545] Temkin, *Misrepresentation by Omission*, 18 Geo. J. Legal Ethics at 180.
[546] Van M. Pounds, *Promoting Truthfulness in Negotiation: A Mindful Approach*, 40 Willamette L. Rev. 181, 189-90 (2004).

I also believe that the rules should include more explicit provisions regarding a lawyer's duty to correct opposing counsel's mistaken factual assumptions. The Committee Notes to Ethical Guideline 4.3.5 state that there is no ethical obligation to correct opposing counsel's erroneous assumptions.[547] Rather, it an implied professional responsibility to correct mistakes induced by the lawyer, since a lawyer has an ethical duty to avoid making misrepresentations.[548] The Ethical Guidelines, however, lack the authority of black letter law and thus are simply aspirational guidelines for lawyers. Ethical Guideline 4.3.5 should be incorporated into the Model Rules because frankly, some lawyers will not go beyond what is legally required of them and will not aspire to maintain high levels of professionalism. Still, lawyers may think twice before failing to correct opposing counsel's mistakes if they are aware that such conduct may amount to an affirmative false statement in violation of Rule 4.1.

When opposing counsel's erroneous assumptions are not induced by the lawyer, I believe that there should be a general rule that a lawyer does not have to correct these mistakes except under limited circumstances, such as where there is a typographical or mathematical error in the settlement agreement. I believe that the Model Rules should include provisions on this matter because otherwise, a disgruntled attorney whose mistake was not corrected has a viable argument under Model Rule 8.4, which provides that a lawyer must not engage in conduct "involving dishonesty, fraud, deceit, or misrepresentation" or that "is prejudicial to the administration of justice." It would be better if this responsibility would be clarified in the rules as to settlement negotiations themselves and not left as an unpredictable inference one might draw from Rule 8.4.

Finally, although the comments to Model Rule 4.1 seem contradictory (since a lawyer generally has no affirmative duty to disclose relevant facts, although under certain circumstances an omission can amount to an overt misrepresentation), I like the idea that there is not a bright line rule, because it leaves room for fairness considerations. On the one hand, a lawyer has a duty to protect his client and preserve his client's trust by maintaining the client's confidences. On the other hand, a lawyer should not be able to hide behind the bounds of client confidentiality when doing so would result in a grave miscarriage of justice. Therefore, the lack of a bright line rule serves to recognize that the duty of zealous advocacy must be balanced against candor and fairness to others.

III. Personal Integrity and Professionalism Considerations

Although failing to disclose certain information in settlement negotiations may not constitute ethical violations, I believe that such a decision must be examined in light of two other equally important considerations: personal integrity and professionalism. As for personal integrity, Professor Charles B. Craver notes:

> Lawyers must remember that they have to live with their own consciences, and not those of their clients or their partners. They must employ tactics they are comfortable using, even in those situations in which other people

---

[547] ABA Section of Litigation, Ethical Guidelines for Settlement Negotiations 56-57 (2002).
[548] *Id.*

> encourage them to employ less reputable behavior. If they adopt techniques they do not consider appropriate, not only will they experience personal discomfort, but they will also fail to achieve their intended objective due to the fact that they will not appear credible when using those tactics. . . . Attorneys should diligently strive to advance client objectives while simultaneously maintaining their personal integrity.[549]

As for professionalism, Professor Craver adds this astute point:

> Untrustworthy advocates encounter substantial difficulty when they negotiate with others. Their oral representations must be verified and reduced to writing, and many opponents distrust their written documents. Their negotiations become especially problematic and cumbersome. If nothing else moves practitioners to behave in an ethical and dignified manner, their hope for long and successful legal careers should induced them to avoid conduct that may undermine their future effectiveness.[550]

Turning to those areas not directly addressed under Model Rule 4.1, I have no qualms about failing to disclose relevant legal authority to opposing counsel during settlement negotiations. A lawyer has a professional obligation to present legal arguments that support his client's position, and also legal arguments that weaken his adversary's position. I believe that I should not be responsible for conducting my own legal research as well as opposing counsel's research. In today's technological age, with the availability of legal databases such as LexisNexis and Westlaw, to my mind there is no excuse for a lawyer to be unaware of applicable legal authority. However, under limited circumstances, I may feel the need to bring legal authority to the attention of opposing counsel, such as if a case had been overturned the day before a settlement conference, or if opposing counsel is relying on information that could lead to an egregious miscarriage of justice.

As far as disclosing relevant facts to opposing counsel who is operating under mistaken facts, I believe that my duty to disclose the mistake depends on the circumstances. If opposing counsel has a mistaken assumption that I helped to create, I would definitely correct the mistake. Although fairness would play a role in the decision, I would mainly disclose in order to protect myself, because my failure to disclose could become the equivalent of an overt misrepresentation, which is prohibited by Rule 4.1. Although I may be protected if I do not incorporate or affirm the mistaken assumptions, I would not want to place myself in a position where I would have to exercise extreme caution to make sure that I do not run afoul of Rule 4.1.

I would be less inclined to correct a mistaken assumption that opposing counsel has that did not derive from me. Although I would not take advantage of transcription or mathematical errors, I would not disclose the mistake if it derives from an outside source, or it is clear that opposing counsel has failed to exercise due diligence in representing his client. I would not feel uncomfortable by failing to correct such mistakes because as mentioned previously, I should not be responsible for doing

---

[549] Craver, *Negotiation Ethics*, 38 S. Tex. L. Rev. at 733.
[550] *Id.* at 734.

work that opposing counsel is obligated (and getting paid) to do. Furthermore, I feel that if opposing counsel is incompetent, his clients have a right to know this, so I would not want to let him off the hook; instead, I would want opposing counsel to have to answer to his clients for his mistakes.

Finally, in terms of distinguishing between a mere lack of disclosure and an overt misrepresentation, I believe that my personal integrity and professionalism views would strongly influence my decision whether to disclose information to opposing counsel, because the Model Rules provide no guideposts for making this determination. I may not have the opportunity to speak with more experienced lawyers or contact my bar's ethics committee to get advice if I am participating in one-day settlement negotiations. Therefore, I would have to decide for myself what would be the most appropriate course of action to take.

This proposition is somewhat uncomfortable. If I make a wrong decision I could jeopardize the settlement and, worse, damage my reputation. However, I am hopeful that my experiences and advice from seasoned lawyers will help me to make a decision that complies with the ethics rule, and is also in harmony with my personal integrity and professionalism views.

IV. Conclusion

As a lawyer, I will inevitably encounter many situations in which the proper course of action will be in black and white. However, studying legal ethics and thinking about my own future in practice has helped me to realize that often times, there will be situations where the proper course of action falls in a grey area. Because the Model Rules are minimalist standards, plenty of questionable behaviors will fall outside of the ethical rules. This is especially true in the settlement negotiations context, because the rules provide less guidance, and less helpful direction, for behavior that takes place outside of the litigation context.

Although certain conduct may not run afoul of the ethics rules, such a determination will not be the end-all for me in deciding the appropriate course of action to take. As a lawyer, I will be sure to balance ethical considerations against personal integrity and professionalism considerations. Although I will zealously advocate for my client to the best of my ability, I will not compromise my own personal morals and risk losing the respect of my colleagues in the legal community. In such a demanding and daunting field such as the legal profession, it seems to me that key to longevity is being prepared and staying true to myself, which I intend to do wholeheartedly.

ABOUT THIS BOOK

Current important events in the U.S. legal profession and legal ethics, with up-to-the-minute research and rules, are explored by Tulane law students from an advanced ethics seminar of spring 2010 and several independent study papers, and by a legal ethics professor in his Foreword. Purchase of this book benefits Tulane PILF, a non-profit student group which funds public interest and indigent client representations throughout the country. Topics include social networking, judicial friends and "friending," and attorney internet advertising; ancillary businesses controlled by lawyers, notably under the latest LMRDA; the Supreme Court's 2009 decision on judicial campaign finance and its implications for judicial selection; and ethics and professionalism in negotiations.

Professors and lawyers with symposia panels of themed works, and conference collections of papers, who want their work to be *out there* fast, and benefit a great cause, should propose editing an addition to the *Benefit Tulane PILF Series*. Papers may still be individually posted or published, and this opportunity does not preclude seeking placing the book eventually with a traditional academic press. Write info@quidprolaw.com and find out how to turn expert panel papers into a themed book, with distribution in paperback and digital formats.

www.quidprolaw.com

www.ingramcontent.com/pod-product-compliance
Lightning Source LLC
Chambersburg PA
CBHW070511090426
42735CB00012B/2738